THE VISION
YESTERDAY and TOMORROW

VISION: YESTERDAY AND TOMORROW. Contains material originally published in magazine form as AVENGERS ICONS: THE VISION #1-4 and AVENGERS #57. Second edition. First printing 2015. ISBN# 978-0-7851-9739-3. Published by MARVEL WORLDWIDE, INC., a subsidiary of MARVEL ENTERTAINMENT, LLC. OFFICE OF PUBLICATION: 135 West 50th Street, New York, NY 10020. **Printed in Canada**. ALAN FINE, EVP - Office of the President, Marvel Worldwide, Inc. and EVP & CMO Marvel Characters B.V.; DAN BUCKLEY, Publisher & President - Print, Animation & Digital Divisions; JOE QUESADA, Chief Creative Officer; TOM BREVOORT, SVP of Publishing; DAVID BOGART, SVP of Operations & Procurement, Publishing; C.B. CEBULSKI, SVP of Creator & Content Development; DAVID GABRIEL, SVP Print, Sales & Marketing; JIM O'KEEFE, VP of Operations & Logistics; DAN CARR, Executive Director of Publishing Technology; SUSAN CRESPI, Editorial Operations Manager; ALEX MORALES, Publishing Operations Manager; STAN LEE, Chairman Emeritus. For information regarding advertising in Marvel Comics or on Marvel.com, please contact Niza Disla, Director of Marvel Partnerships, at ndisla@marvel.com. For Marvel subscription inquiries, please call 800-217-9158. **Manufactured between 2/27/2015 and 4/6/2015 by SOLISCO PRINTERS, SCOTT, QC, CANADA.**

10 9 8 7 6 5 4 3 2 1

COLORS: CHRIS SOTOMAYOR
LETTERS: PAUL TUTRONE

AVENGERS #57
WRITER: ROY THOMAS
PENCILER: JOHN BUSCEMA

INKER: GEORGE KLEIN
LETTERS: SAM ROSEN

WRITER: GEOFF JOHNS
PENCILER: IVAN REIS
INKERS: JOE PIMENTEL & OCLAIR ALBERT

ASSISTANT EDITORS: MARC SUMERAK & ANDY SCHMIDT
EDITOR: TOM BREVOORT
COVER ART: BRIAN HABERLIN

COLLECTION EDITOR: MARK D. BEAZLEY
ASSISTANT MANAGING EDITOR: JOE HOCHSTEIN
ASSOCIATE MANAGING EDITOR: ALEX STARBUCK

EDITOR, SPECIAL PROJECTS: JENNIFER GRÜNWALD
SENIOR EDITOR, SPECIAL PROJECTS: JEFF YOUNGQUIST
MASTERWORKS EDITOR: CORY SEDLMEIER

BOOK DESIGNER: CARRIE BEADLE
SVP PRINT, SALES & MARKETING: DAVID GABRIEL

EDITOR IN CHIEF: AXEL ALONSO
CHIEF CREATIVE OFFICER: JOE QUESADA
PUBLISHER: DAN BUCKLEY
EXECUTIVE PRODUCER: ALAN FINE

HABERLIN
#1

Can you see the future?
FASSHT!
It's right in front of us.
PRESS
Looks like a Utopia. Whatta you guys think?
I think the World of Tomorrow is going to be perfect.
FASSHT!

QUEENS, NEW YORK.
AUGUST 31ST, 1939.

Yesterday
and
Tomorrow
GEOFF JOHNS WRITER
IVAN REIS PENCILER
JOE PIMENTAL INKER
CHRIS SOTOMAYOR COLORIST
PAUL TUTRONE LETTERER
MARC SUMERAK &
ANDY SCHMIDT ASST. EDITORS
TOM BREVOORT EDITOR
JOE QUESADA EDITOR IN CHIEF
BILL JEMAS PRESIDENT

You believe that line? Folks must be waitin' for hours.
Everyone wants to feel optimistic. 'Specially with all the rumbling over in Europe. Heck, Roosevelt's dedication speech was basically "Germany -- please play nice."
Aw, yer worryin' too much.
In any case, thank La Guardia for these press passes.
PRESS
PRESS
Thank the Mayor for a lot of things. Like the tip on this scientist guy.
Says he could be the next Einstein.
Right. Heard that before.
Where is this fella anyway? His setup's supposed to be around here some--
Hey, kid!
We're lookin' for a professor. Professor Phineas T. Horton.
Yeah. You know where he is?
Do I know where he is? Of course, I know where he is.
I'm Professor Horton!

AHA HAHAHA! HA!

Right, kid.

C'mon, guys. We got a *lotta* ground ta cover.

Wait! I *am* Horton. And what I'm going to show you...

What I'm going to show you will make all these dreams of *passenger airships* and *super highways* look like *tiddlywinks!*

--*aheemm*--

--the *vision of tomorrow!*
Looks like the *Tin Man* from *Oz.*
What *is* that? Some kinda *robot?*
FASSHT!
No. It's much *more* than a robot.
It can *think.*
KLIK
Think? What do you--
With *this.*

I call it a solar gem. An invention of my own design.
Combined with the solar epidermal covering its body, the gem focuses sunlight, converts it and distributes the energy evenly throughout.
The gem works like a human brain... but hundreds of times more powerful.
"The promise of the future is still greater than all the glories of the past." And for all you writing that down--
--Phineas is with a "P.H."
Can it talk?
No. Not yet... but it can walk. A demonstration.
Come over to me.
It's not doin' nothin'.
Ah, this is just a bunch of--
I'll be.
KZZZZ
Will ya look at that! It's--
SSKRRT!

S'on fire!
BWOOOSH!
Oh, no! Nononono.
Not again!
SPWOOSH!

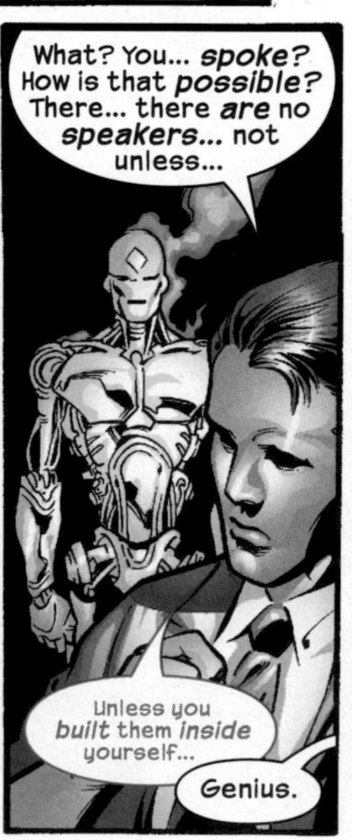

You are a genius, Professor Horton. There can be no doubt.
I... thought you all left.
But you aren't appreciated here. You're ignored.

You deserve to be honored, well-funded... and well-rewarded. Tell me, Professor--
--have you ever considered moving to Berlin?
PRESS

Wha--
I know who you work for...
Get out.

I have seen tomorrow, Professor. You will be a part of it, like it or not.
Auf Wiedersehen.

I'll be a part of nothing like--
The gem! He took the other--

Go stop him! Stop him!
Come on, you stupid--

No! Where did he--
Help! Somebody help! Somebody--

WHUPP!
WHUP
WHUP
WHUP!

QUEENS, NEW YORK.
TODAY.
WHUP
WHUP
I-98
298

WHUP!
PALACE
SEX
OÏA EU AQUI
OCLAIR

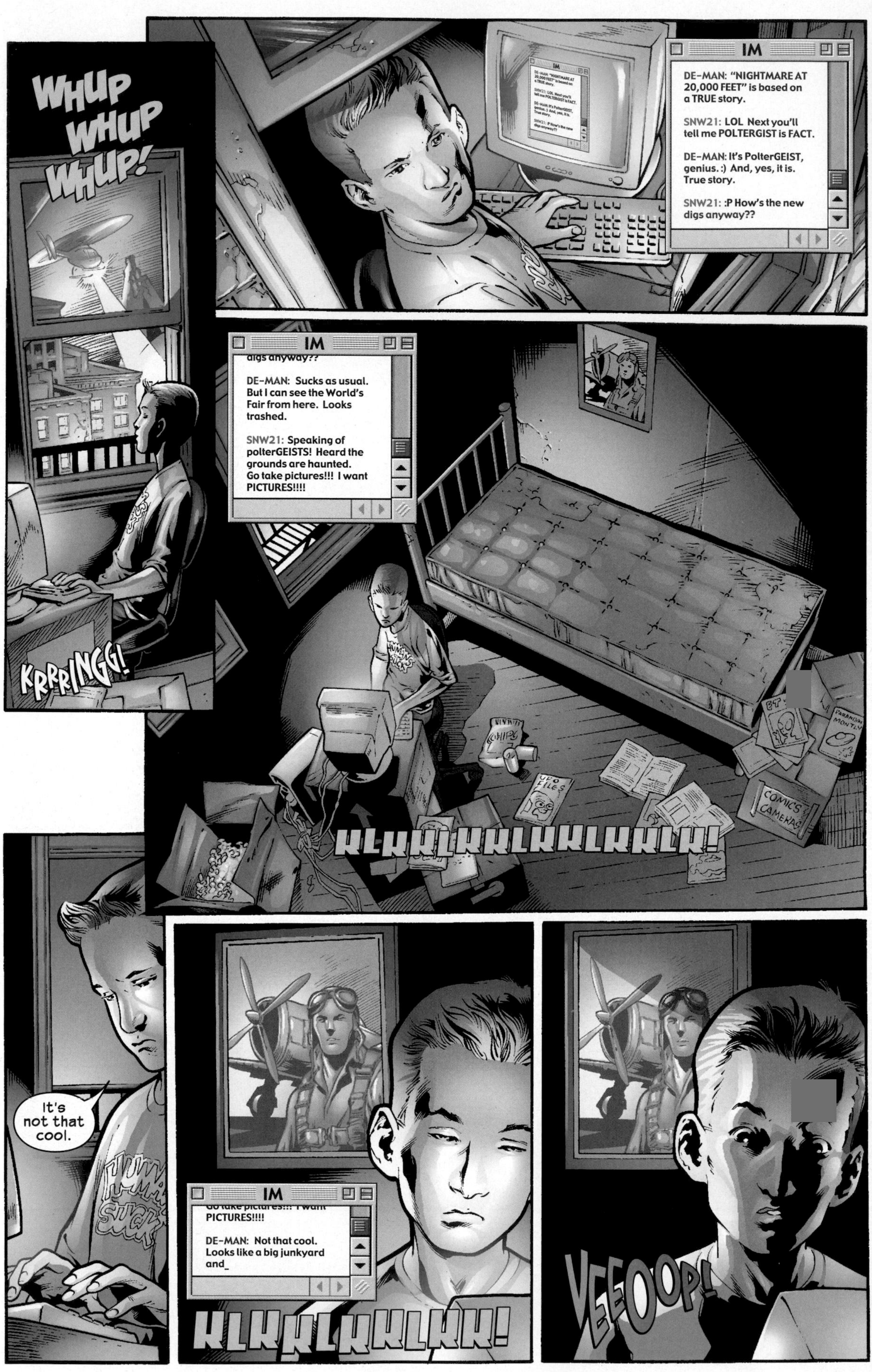
WHUP WHUP WHUP!
KRRRINGG!
IM
DE-MAN: "NIGHTMARE AT 20,000 FEET" is based on a TRUE story.
SNW21: LOL Next you'll tell me POLTERGIST is FACT.
DE-MAN: It's PolterGEIST, genius. :) And, yes, it is. True story.
SNW21: :P How's the new digs anyway??
IM
digs anyway??
DE-MAN: Sucks as usual. But I can see the World's Fair from here. Looks trashed.
SNW21: Speaking of polterGEISTS! Heard the grounds are haunted. Go take pictures!!! I want PICTURES!!!!
KLKKLKKLKKLKKLK!
It's not that cool.
IM
Go take pictures!!! I want PICTURES!!!!
DE-MAN: Not that cool. Looks like a big junkyard and_
KLKKLKKLKK!
VEEOOP!

Dad! I was talking to someone.
Dammit, Derek! The whole block is having electrical problems. I told you we're not supposed to plug anything in.
You want to cause a blackout?
You could've at least asked me to turn it off. I didn't even get to say "bye."
To your on-line friends? We moved in twenty minutes ago and you're already on the computer. Chatting.
I.M.-ing
Whatever. You need to tear yourself away from that fantasy world. Make some real friends for once.
UFO FILES MAGAZINE
DETROIT LIONS

Kinda hard when you're moving every four months.

Hey.
I go where I have to. Where the Air Force needs me. It's not easy trying to raise a kid and juggle a career in the military--
A desk job you mean. Doin' what? Designing landing gear and decals?

It's not like you're Captain America... or even Grandpa. He was a real soldier. A real pilot.
'Til the gremlins got him.

Stop with the science fiction crap. It was an engine failure not a--
But Mom said--

Mom wasn't thinking right, Derek! Not for her last few years!
She wasn't--

DETROIT LIONS

Look, son...
I'm going to try and stay here-- stay in Queens-- permanently. No more moving. No more new schools. I'm really going to try.
Okay?

Yeah.
Sorry, dad.

I'll... I'll see you tomorrow.

HUMANS SUCK
UFO

KZZZATTT!

Dad?

Yesterday Is tomorrow.

Wha--?

Must've been *dreaming* or--

KZZAT

PARANORMA
MAGAZINE
THE GHOSTS OF YESTERDAY

CAMERA

WHUP WHUP
WHUP WHUP
Wonder what that helicopter's looking for.

Say *cheese.*

FASSHT!
Yesterday.

Uh...
Hello?

Ah, whatever. There's no one--

Tomorrow.

SKRRUTCH

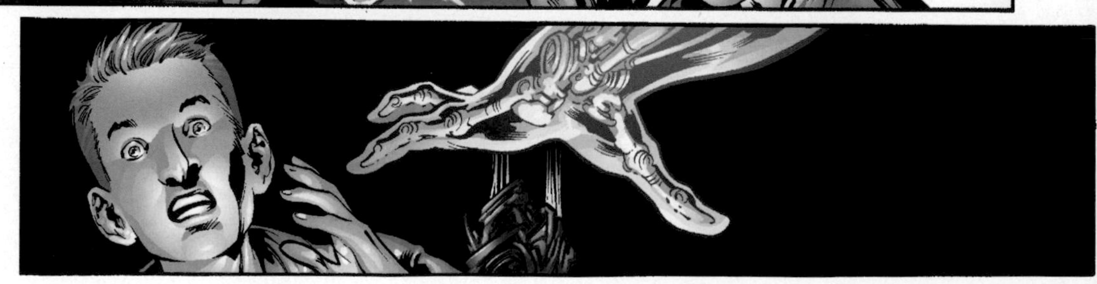

Help! Dad!

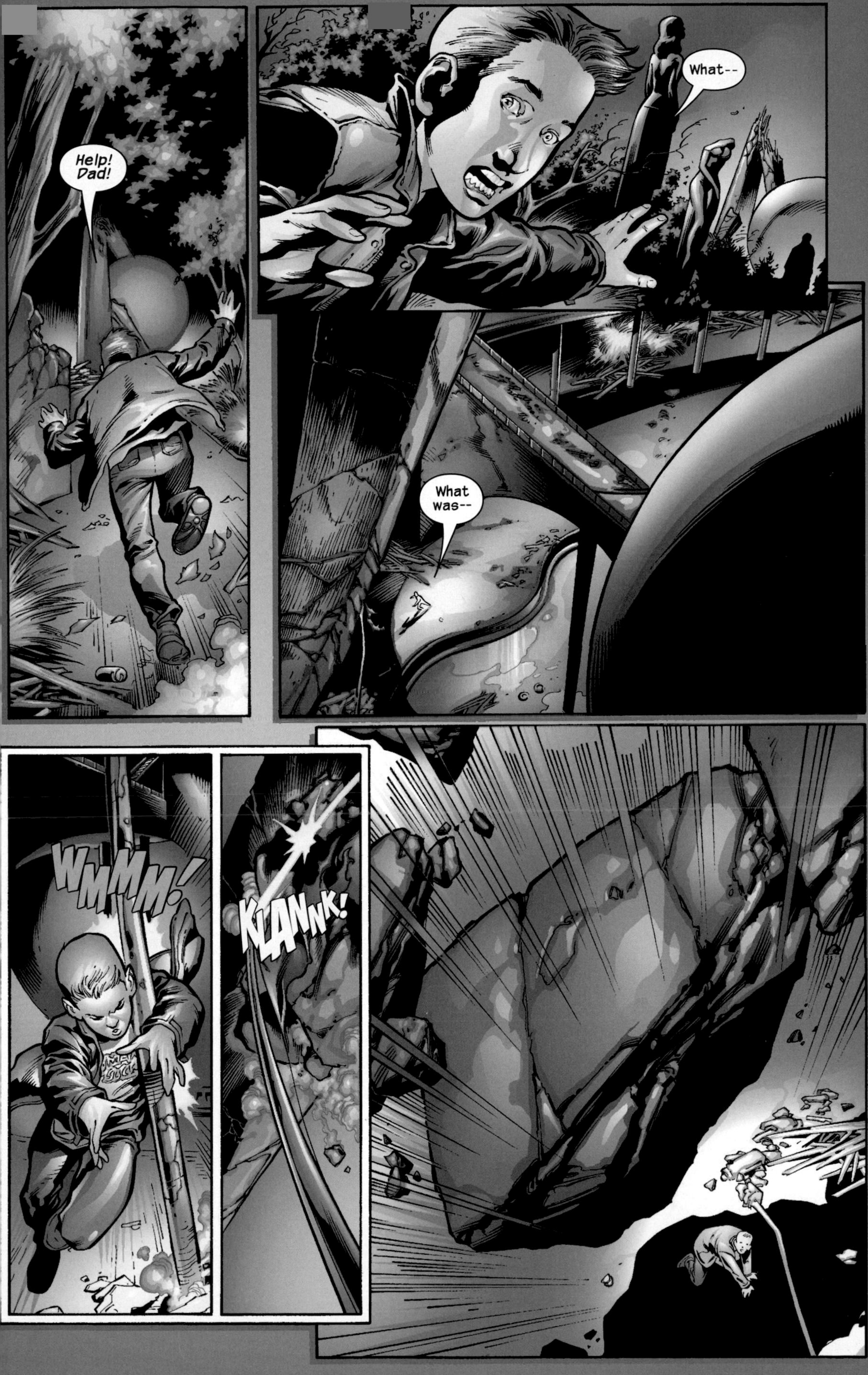

What--
What was--

WMMM!
KLANNK!

AAAI!

ZEE

ZZEEEOOOO!
ZZZZZEEEEEKKOOOOOMM!

HFF! HFFF!
Unn. Place...
VVV
Place is haunted.
It's--
NNFF! Ow.
It's real.
Whatever you are, stay the hell away from me!

I am *the vision* of *tomorrow*.
TO BE CONTINUED

#2

Why didn't you obey me?

I was supposed to be famous, damn you! I was supposed to be a hero like Einstein and Ford-- not a traitor! Oh, God--

--I was supposed to be a hero.
I have to stop it.

Stop it? What are you talking about? What--
What are you, man?!

I am not a man.
HUMANS SUCK

In 1939, the world's first artificial intelligence was created. Years later, the android was rediscovered, rebuilt with the ability to become ephemeral as a ghost or hard as a diamond, and programmed to destroy America's greatest champions. But the android refused, and instead joined the ranks of Earth's Mightiest Heroes himself. Not quite human, much more than a machine. Stan Lee Presents THE VISION!

EYE OF THE BEHOLDER

GEOFF JOHNS WRITER
IVAN REIS PENCILER
JOE PIMENTAL INKER
CHRIS SOTOMAYOR COLORIST
PAUL TUTRONE LETTERER
MARC SUMERAK & ANDY SCHMIDT ASST. EDITORS
TOM BREVOORT EDITOR
JOE QUESADA EDITOR IN CHIEF
BILL JEMAS PRESIDENT

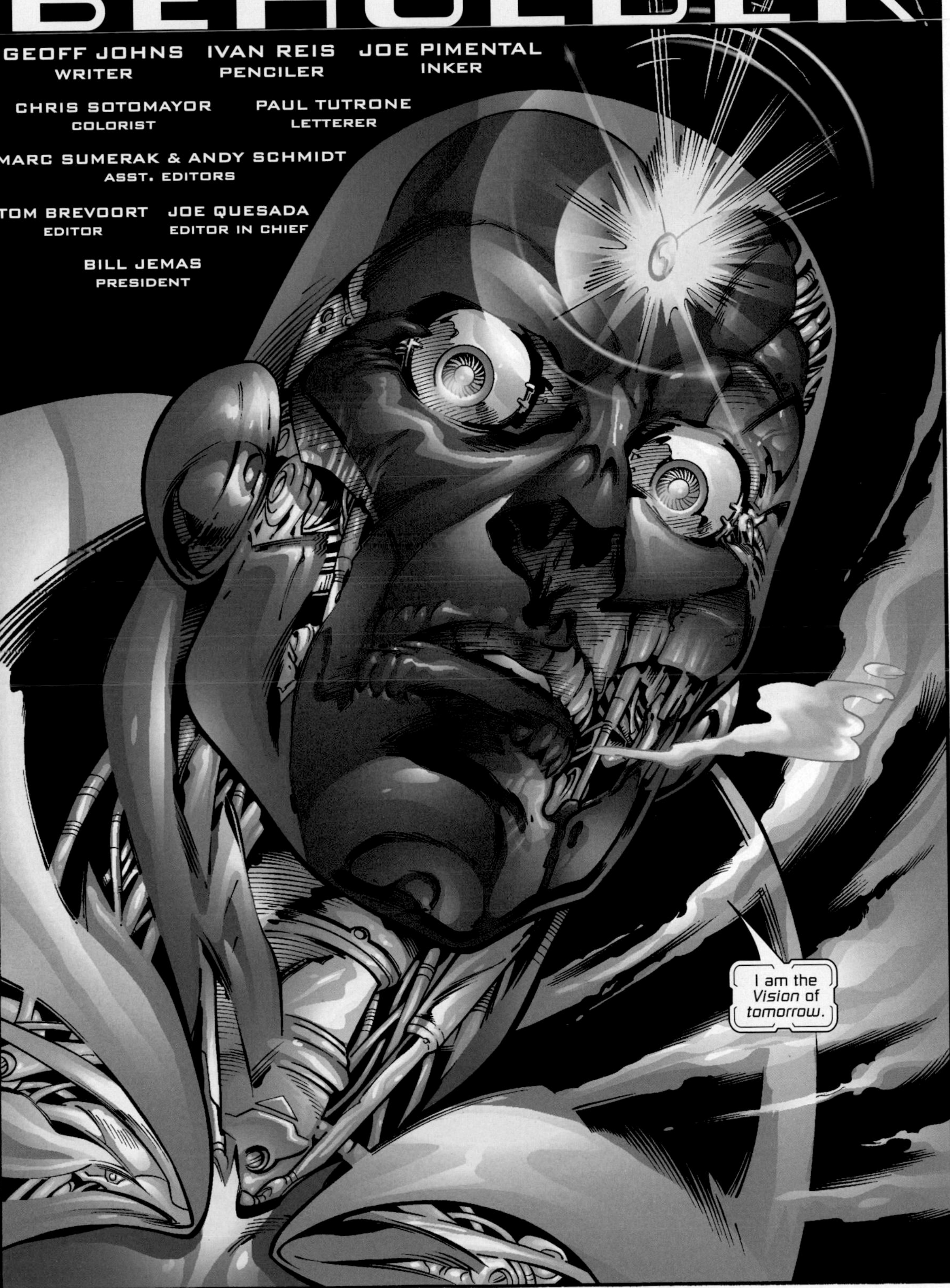

What do you want?!
HUMANS SUCK
My camera... but you turned it into scrap.
How'd you fix it?
KRRKK!
Hey!
VZZH
VRR
No way.

You're not a *ghost*, are you?
Ghosts do not exist.
I am a *synthezoid*.
A robot...?
You're... *cold*.
I will adjust my temperature core to reflect that of yours.
Ninety-eight point six four two degrees Fahrenheit.
VZZZH
I have forgotten how relative and unsettling temperature can be.
I have forgotten *many* things.

My memory has been downloaded and stolen. My thoughts torn from me.
I recall my earliest days with him, but little else.
Him who?
My creator. Professor Phineas T. Horton. I have come *home* to the fair-grounds to seek him out.
I must stop what I failed to stop.

You're looking for Phineas Horton?

You found him.

PHINEAS T. HORTON
BRILLIANT SCIENTIST
BELOVED GRANDFATHER
TOMORROW IS FOREVER

That is a stone.
It's his grave.
It means he...
He died.

Thanks for giving me a future. Love, Victoria

FWASSHHTTT!

WHUPP
WHUPP
WHUPP
WHUPP!

WHUPP
WHUPP
WHUPP!
It has found me.
What? What has?
A mistake.

WHUPP
WHUPP
WHUPP!

SWK

FFFTFFFTFFTFFFT!
Your heart rate has increased, your breathing erratic. Why do you panic?
Are you kidding? It's *shooting* at us!
VVTT
VVTT
VVTT!
You feel *fear?*
ZMM!
VZZZHH!
WHUPPWHUPP! WHUU--
Fear is an *invalid* emotion. Ignited in human behavior by ignorance and an absence of confidence.

BRAAKKA-BOOOMMMM!
I fear nothing.
--unit fifty-seven responding. Looks like a helicopter went down! I repeat--
What the hell was...
Derek?
DO YOU BELIEVE?

HFF HFFF.
SKRREEEEEE
Don't move! Don't--
Just a kid.
Get outta there! Fire Department is on its--
What... what the heck is *that?*
SSHFF
Doug! Watch--
SKREEEEE
HUMANS SUCK
FWMMPPP
RRRRRMMMMM

HHN!
Do not struggle.
You may get damaged.
KRRKKAKK!
KRRKASSHHH!

The cops--?
Those humans are still breathing. Hearts still beating.

KRRRSHHHK!

The... the car just *started* up by itself!
This is unfortunate.
VRRROOOMM!

KRRRTCHHH!

VRRROOOOOOO!
It is still watching us.
I have to leave.
VIZZZH
VVZZZHHHRRAAKK!
KRRKRAKOOOOMMM!

You can't just *steal* my dad's car!
My end-program is more important than the ownership of this inanimate machine.
VEET
SVRRK
RRRUMMm
Where are you going?
I must perform a search, find the one person that may truly help me. And I must hunt for this human without technology.
If I access any computer system, make any phone call, the Gremlin will track me.
Gremlin?

I'm... I'm coming with you.
This does not concern you.

It does now.
DEREK!
HUMANS SUCK
CHKK

Derek!!

TKK
TKKTKK
TKK

VEEEE
I know you are here.
I can sense you.

WHPPWHPPPZZ
No. My... memory cells. Get out of my--

ARRZZZZZZZ

VEEEE
I know you are here.
I can sense you.

WHPPWHPPPZZ
No. My... memory cells. Get out of my--

Hello?

Someone in here?
KIKK KIKK KIKK

Are you going to talk to me?
For what purpose?
Can you tell me where we are?

My birthplace.

The Professor stored all of his records at his home. He refused to keep personal data on computers--
KREEEK
--because he was betrayed too many times by technology.

And by humans.
He told me, long ago, if this mistake emerged his next of kin would have the solution.

What are we looking for?
Information directing us to the owner of this card. This "Victoria." Perhaps she is the one I seek.
Door's locked.

AA!

Don't *do* that. You're freaking me out...
I told you before. Fear is an invalid emotion.
KLKK

You know...
You haven't even asked me my name.

SRRRPP

It's *Derek.*

Look at all this. A scrapbook.

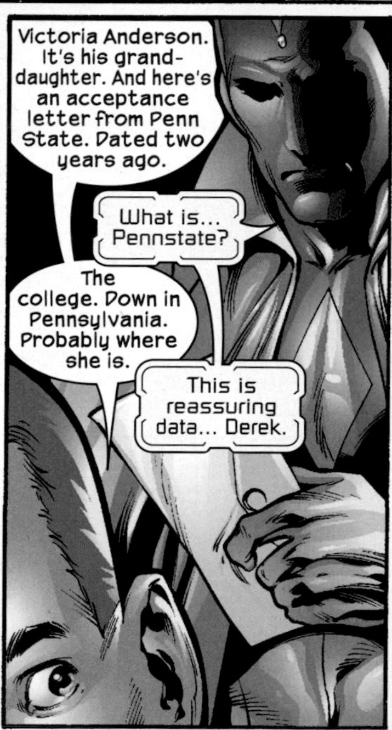
Victoria Anderson. It's his granddaughter. And here's an acceptance letter from Penn State. Dated two years ago.
What is... Pennstate?
The college. Down in Pennsylvania. Probably where she is.
This is reassuring data... Derek.

Victoria may hold the key to stopping the Gremlin. To correcting my mistake.
My creator promised me that all of his offspring, and theirs--

"—would be as studious and brilliant as him."
PENN STATE.
Watch out!
Hey!
FWMPP!
I said watch out.
Victoria! Over here!
Hey, Tina.
Where you off to?
Late again. See you tonight, right? Keg stands?
It *is* Tuesday.
Denny!
Hi, Victoria.
Don't you look cute today.
Hey, I was wondering if I could borrow your Engineering notes from yesterday. Oh, and Friday too... all last week in fact.
I was *really* busy with other stuff.

--many questions about what *artificial intelligence* actually means. It boils down to one thing.

Computers that can *learn* from their *mistakes.*

And the other aspect of artificial intelligence we'll be discussing this week-- as computers begin to *think* and create specific information algorithms-- it may lead to a better understanding of *human* learning as well.

Machines learn from humans. Humans learn from machines.

ALGORITHMS IN COMPUTERS AND HUMANS

It's all rather fascinating, isn't it?

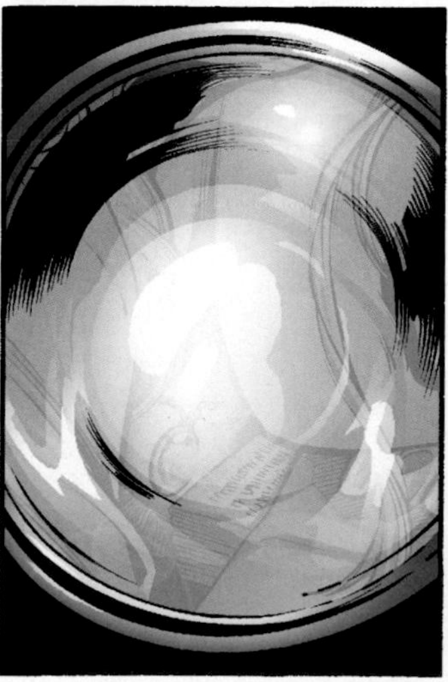

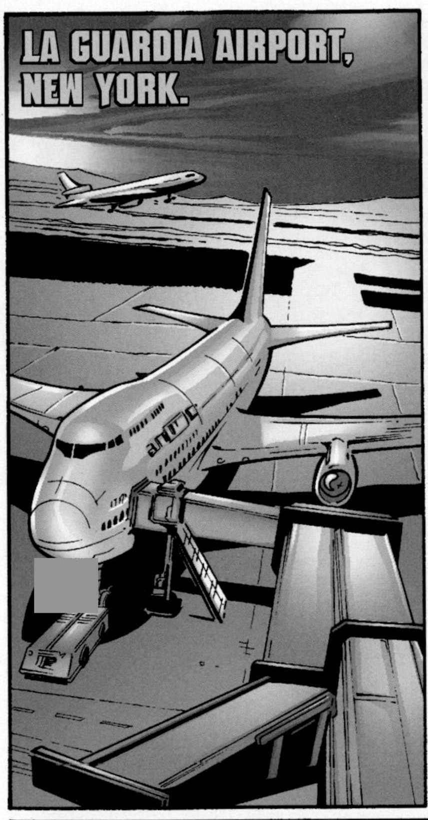
LA GUARDIA AIRPORT, NEW YORK.

--departing for University Park, Pennsylvania. Gate thirteen.

Flight crew, prepare for take off.
KNKKNKK

RRRREEEEEEE

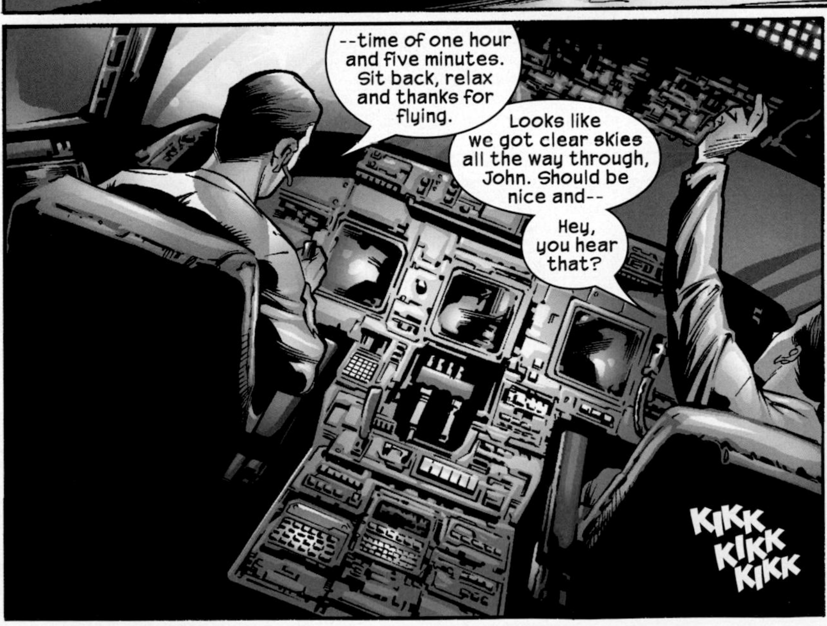
--time of one hour and five minutes. Sit back, relax and thanks for flying.
Looks like we got clear skies all the way through, John. Should be nice and--
Hey, you hear that?
KIKK KIKK KIKK

KIKK KIKK KIKK KIKK
What is that?

KREEEKK

SHNKK!

SPPTTT

AAAA!

SHEEEEKK

HNF

--and the World of Tomorrow will belong to the Gremlin.
TO BE CONTINUED

#3

Flight 57, this is University Park Tower--
--you are cleared for landing.
SNAPP!
KRSSHTT!
AAH!
What--
--God! What the hell is--
KZZZZTTTT

In 1939, the world's first artificial intelligence was created. Years later, the android was rediscovered, rebuilt with the ability to become ephemeral as a ghost or hard as a diamond, and programmed to destroy America's greatest champions. But the android refused, and instead joined the ranks of Earth's Mightiest Heroes himself. Not quite human, much more than a machine. Stan Lee Presents THE VISION!

GEOFF JOHNS writer IVAN REIS penciler JOE PIMENTEL inker
CHRIS SOTOMAYOR colorist PAUL TUTRONE letterer
MARC SUMERAK & ANDY SCHMIDT asst. editors TOM BREVOORT editor
JOE QUESADA editor in chief BILL JEMAS president

PENN STATE
NEXT RIGHT
UNIVERSITY PARK
AIR FORCE BASE
2 MILES
Sometimes I can hear her talking to me.
VROOOOO
I know it's weird, but when people die that just can't be all there is.
I think their spirits continue on. Watching over us. Like my mom.
MAPS
Do you believe in ghosts?
MAPS
No.
VMMMM
We are close.
RRMMMMM
Close to finding the only one that can help us—

DRINK! DRINK! DRINK!
"—Victoria Anderson.
"Granddaughter of the greatest scientific mind in history."
Whoa. Head rush.
Hey, Dave. Studying robotics?
Hate that class.
SPLLSHT
Why ya takin' it?
My grandfather. Never met him, but the money he left me-- his will said it'd only pay my way through school if I majored in Robotic Engineering.
Gave me a future, I guess--
--and this.
...I like it.

HEY!
That wasn't an invitation!

God. Real nice.
Dave is dissed.
I live for it.

Jerk.
Is *this* what you wanted?
To make your granddaughter miserable?
What--?
VIZZH

AAAAA!
Hello, Victoria Anderson.
Get the hell away!
Get--

I told him not to rush in.
He's not good with patience--
--or people.
I'm Derek Hoffman, by the way.
I drank too much... that's all. I just--
Your grandfather was my creator, Victoria. Now I must ask with haste, as we have limited time.
My memory cells have been damaged, my nanite-nerve mesh scrambled. Can you repair it?
VIZH
What?

WHUPPWHUPPWHUPPWHUPP!
Hang on, Mr. Hoffman.

Sergeant Briggs here.
You're one of the A.F.'s most important engineers, Mr. Hoffman.
I appreciate the ride. And the help in finding my son. I know this is personal but--
Hell, the work you've done on reconfiguring the B-1B's landing gear has saved more lives than anyone can count. We'll give you whatever you need.

Sat did a visual trace on your car, followed it here. In the middle of Penn State's campus.
You're sure you don't want assistance? Military or local police?
I don't know why he took the car for a joyride but... I'd like to take care of this myself. Before he gets in real tr--
KIKK KIKK
KIKK

--what's wrong with your--
KIKK KIKK
KIKK

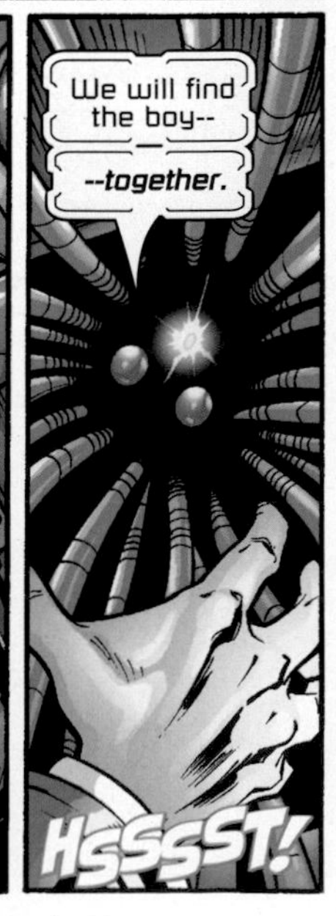
We will find the boy--
--together.
HSSSST!

Something tells me she's not exactly *following* in her grandfather's *footsteps.*
Victoria Anderson.
I'd take it *real* slow, Vision.

You must help us.
Don't touch me!

Yeah. *That's* taking it *slow.*

FWASHT!

FWASSHHT!

FFZZZZZMMMM!

Hello, children.

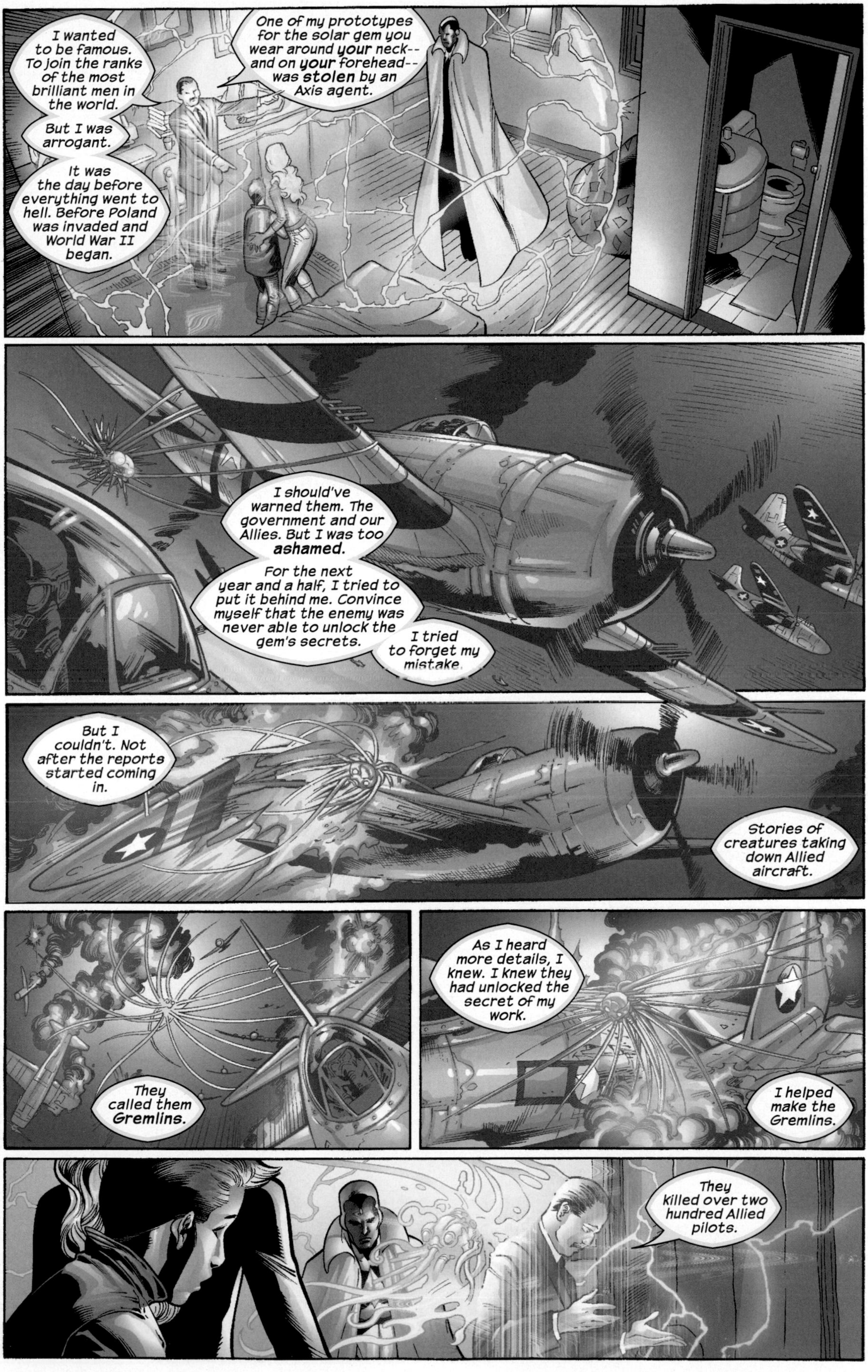

I wanted to be famous. To join the ranks of the most brilliant men in the world.
But I was arrogant.
It was the day before everything went to hell. Before Poland was invaded and World War II began.
One of my prototypes for the solar gem you wear around **your** neck-- and on **your** forehead-- was **stolen** by an Axis agent.
I should've warned them. The government and our Allies. But I was too **ashamed.**
For the next year and a half, I tried to put it behind me. Convince myself that the enemy was never able to unlock the gem's secrets.
I tried to forget my mistake.
But I couldn't. Not after the reports started coming in.
Stories of creatures taking down Allied aircraft.
They called them **Gremlins.**
As I heard more details, I knew. I knew they had unlocked the secret of my work.
I helped make the Gremlins.

They killed over two hundred Allied pilots.

I made it my mission to see those Gremlins turned into scrap, never telling anyone why.
Working with the heroes of that era, the Allies destroyed them.

All but one. The "leader" who controlled the others. Powered by my stolen gem.
It was captured by the Russians. Held for decades in Northern Siberia.

But eventually it escaped.

A month ago, a plane from Berlin crashed on the East Coast. Details were sketchy until the black box was recovered.
And my worst fears were realized. The Gremlin had come back to America, hoping to complete its mission.
To terrorize the United States from the skies.

It's already come after me once... and I suspect I won't **survive** my next close encounter.
I spent my life trying to keep track of it, trying to dismantle it... I'll die trying...
Which is why I made this message, children. Only activated when the two of you meet.
You **must** find the Gremlin, remove the gem--
--and destroy it.

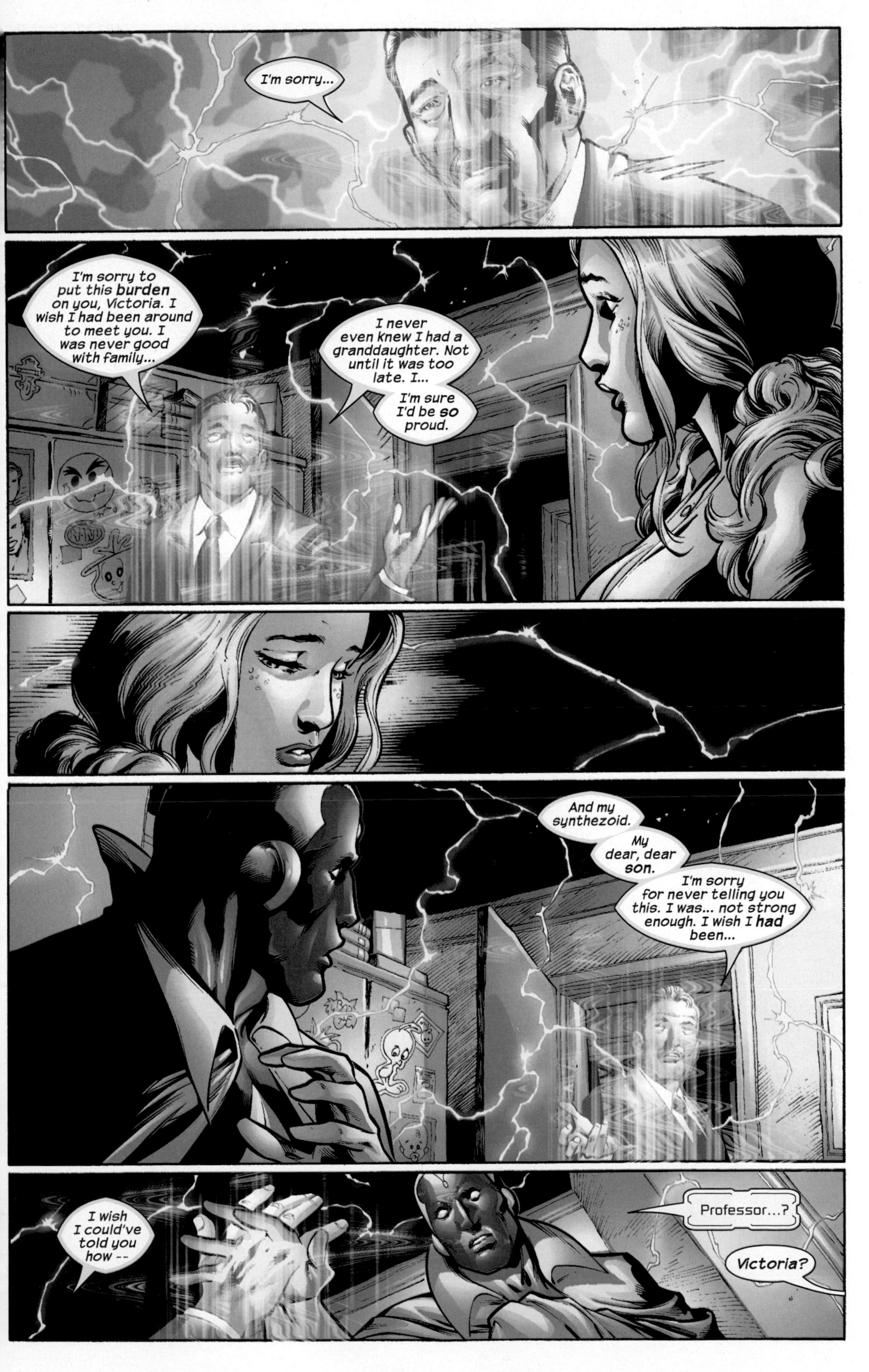
I'm sorry...
I'm sorry to put this burden on you, Victoria. I wish I had been around to meet you. I was never good with family...
I never even knew I had a granddaughter. Not until it was too late. I...
I'm sure I'd be so proud.
And my synthezoid.
My dear, dear son.
I'm sorry for never telling you this. I was... not strong enough. I wish I had been...
I wish I could've told you how --
Professor...?
Victoria?

Victoria! Give me a second ch--
FZZZAAPP!
FZZP
What the hell?
No.
Come back.
Father.
You have no manners, human.
So I will teach you some.
Don't! Don't hurt him!
FWMMP

Somebody, help!
Victoria!
Wait!
VIZZH
Humans.
Go home.
PEN

Come on.
Keyskeyskeys.
Wait a second!

Didn't you hear all that? What your grandfather said?
This is not happening.
HUMANS SUCK
Yes, it is. And that thing killed my grandfather. He was one of those pilots.
But what can I do? I'm not like my grandfather...

I'm not smart, okay?

FMMP
The locks! They--

VRRROOMM

Oh, terrific!

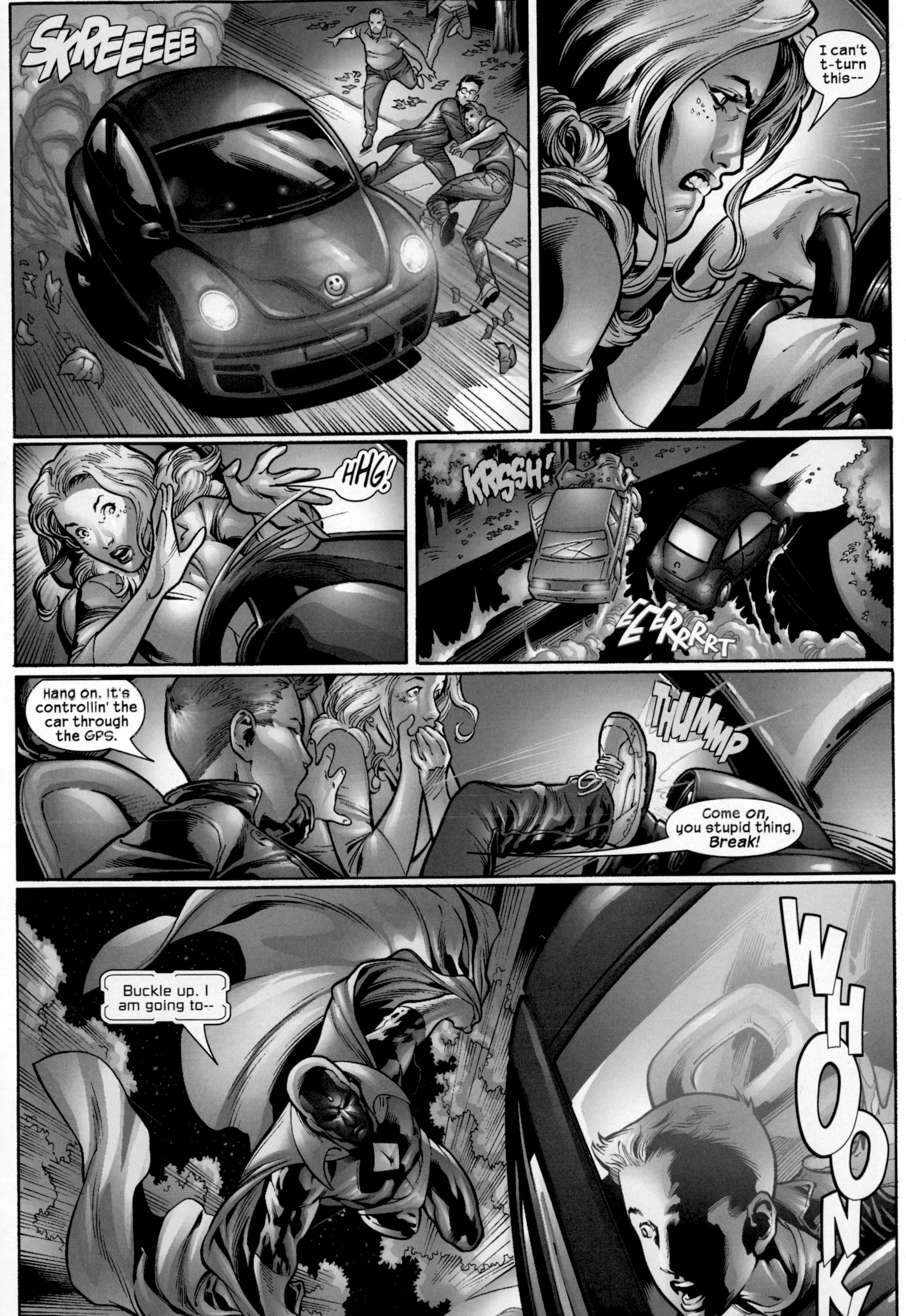

SKREEEEEE
I can't t-turn this--
HHG!
KRSSH!
EEERRRRT
Hang on. It's controllin' the car through the GPS.
THUMMP
Come on, you stupid thing. Break!
Buckle up. I am going to--
WHOONK!

WHOOOOONK!

UNIVERSITY PARK AIR FORCE BASE
STOP
KANGGSHT!!
VRROOOO

VREEETT

UHN!

KRRANKKSHHH!
HUMANS SUCK

AHH!
Derek!
FWAPP

D-Dad?
Did you bring the android?
Gremlin.
Let the boy and his father go.
I am prepared this time to finish the task. To wipe your circuits clean... and have you join me.
Do you feel it yet?
What?
FVMMMMM
KLAKK KLAKK

Fear, my brother.
Do you feel fear?
Never.
TO BE CONCLUDED.

#4

You have been infected by humans.
Let me access your solar gem. I will finish reprogramming your memory cells. I will erase your humanity.
You cannot erase that.
My humanity comes from them.
But I can and will erase it, brother.
Even if it is one American at a time.
Vision!
Victoria. Get clear.
HEY!
WHRRRRRR
WHRT

In 1939, the world's first artificial intelligence was created. Years later, the android was rediscovered, rebuilt with the ability to become ephemeral as a ghost or hard as a diamond, and programmed to destroy America's greatest champions. But the android refused, and instead joined the ranks of Earth's Mightiest Heroes himself. Not quite human, much more than a machine. Stan Lee Presents THE VISION!
DOGFIGHT
GEOFF JOHNS writer IVAN REIS penciler ALBERT & PIMENTEL inkers
CHRIS SOTOMAYOR colorist PAUL TUTRONE letterer
MARC SUMERAK & ANDY SCHMIDT asst. editors TOM BREVOORT editor
JOE QUESADA editor in chief BILL JEMAS president
CHOOOMMMM!

CHOOOMMM!

Come now.
Ow! Ease off, cyber-freak.
It is time for more terror.

BAABOOOMM!

KAAMM!
VIZHHH!

Let my dad go.
However, inside, information or not, he is like every other human.
Confused.
This host is the tool that will allow me to pilot the B-52 Stratofortress.
AA.
W-Why are you doing this? What's the point?
The point?
I had assumed you were intelligent, Victoria Anderson. Your grand-father did create me.
The point, child, is to follow my program.
You humans have no set program to follow. Which is why you make mistakes. You... wander.
My program is to create as much fear and death on American soil as my abilities allow. To rain it down from the sky. I will carry this objective out with-out question or confusion.
And when you are all gone—
"—my brother will join me—
VVVVVVVVVVVVVV!

"—or be dismantled."
VVVVVVVVV
CHINK CHINK CHINK
Machines.
Machines cannot stop me.
I am *more* than a *machine*.
KRRRANK!

PHILADELPHIA

HONK HONK!

Hey! That's *my* cab!

WHONKK!

VVVVVVVVVVVVVVV

There's no way my grandfather made... something *like* you. You're just... I think you're a reject of his. A failed experiment.

It is the Vision who is the failed experiment, not—

KRRSHHT!

UHH·

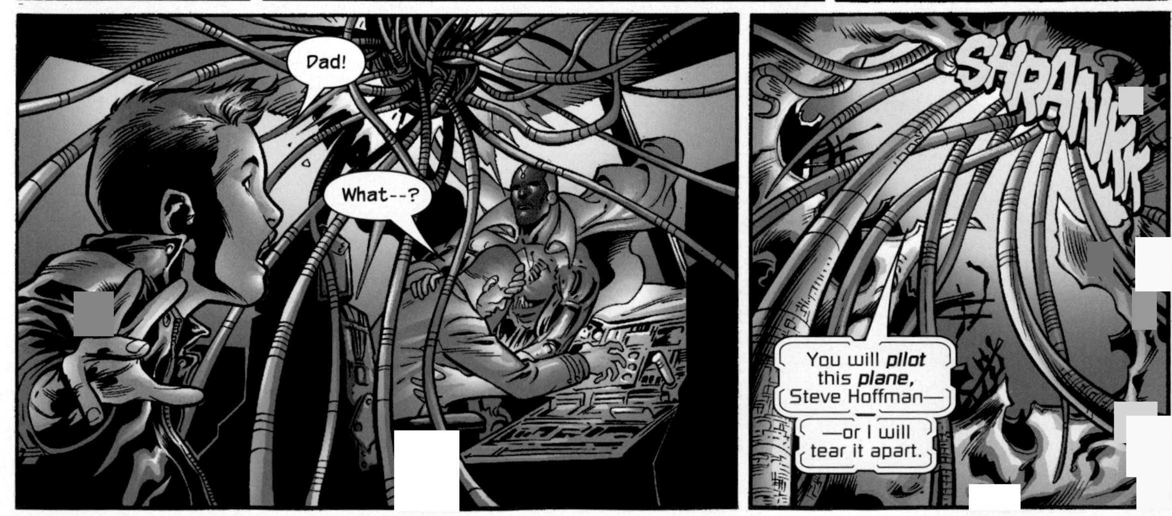

TKK TKKTKK
Fall.
No, Gremlin.
FZZZZZZ
KZZZT

I will not let them.
FZZZZZZ
You have fused the bombs in place—
—then you have sealed the fate of these humans.
This entire plane must go down.
You first.
SKATCHH!

How'd he do that? Take out the control panel...
He can shift his density... be like a ghost.
Or like diamond.

Dad! The Gremlin's trying to make us *crash*. Right in the city. With the bombs--
I know, Derek. But the landing gear release isn't working...
I need you to get under the dash. Find the manual emergency.

Are we going to die?

KRAANNNK

VISION!
TUNK TUNK TUNK!
I've gotta be craz-- OW!
VISION!
Victoria. Get inside.
Wait! Listen to me!
Let that thing assimilate you!
What?
You can--

I have you now—
—brother.

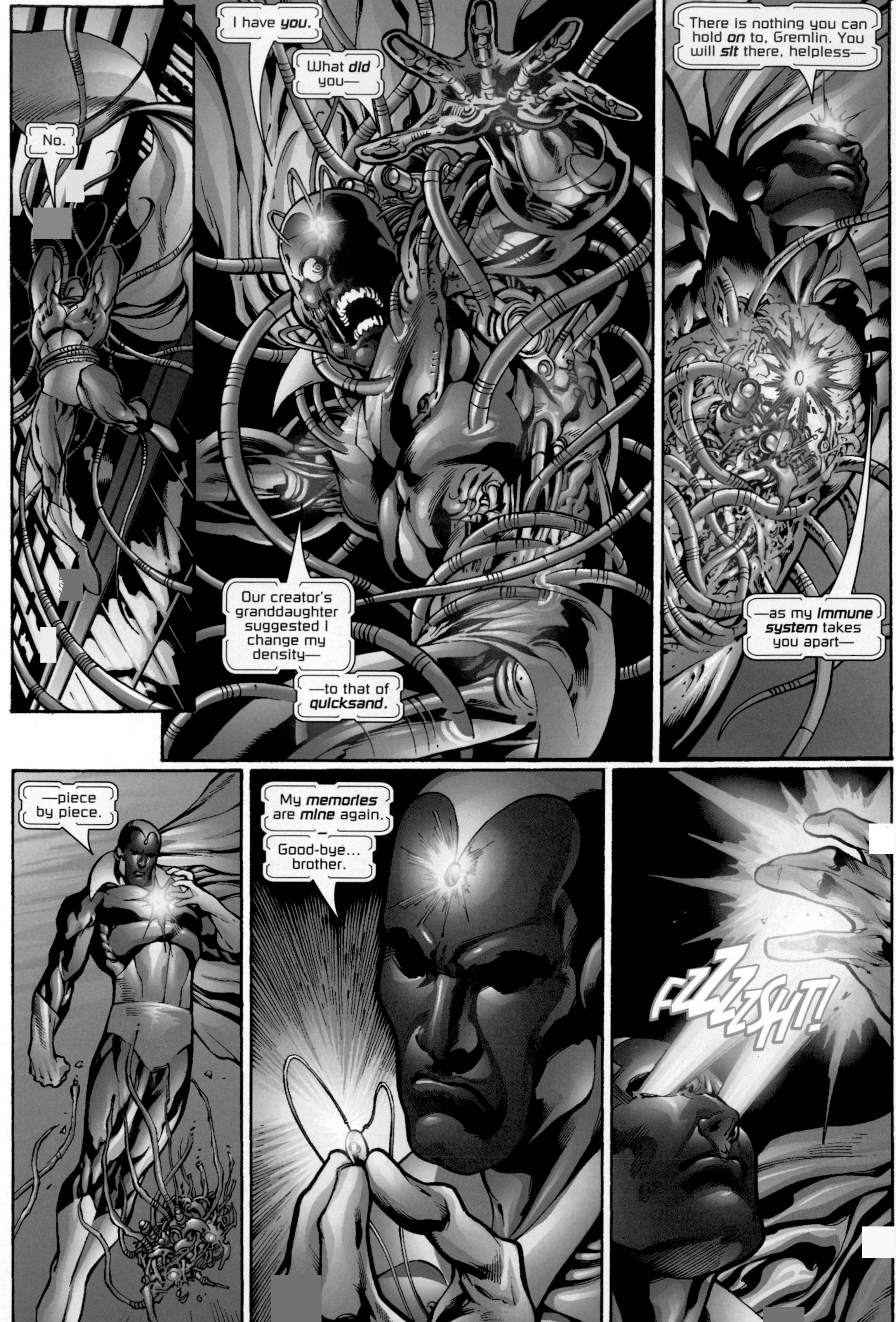

No.
I have you.
What did you—
Our creator's granddaughter suggested I change my density—
—to that of quicksand.
There is nothing you can hold on to, Gremlin. You will sit there, helpless—
—as my immune system takes you apart—
—piece by piece.
My memories are mine again.
Good-bye... brother.
FZZZZSHT!

SKRRRP

WHRRR

There, Derek! You got it!
And the Gremlin is gone—
—thanks to Victoria Anderson.
It was just an idea.

With my memories down-loaded and my full abilities returned, I was able to send out a signal through my internal communications array.
The end of Highway 95 North will be cleared for landing.
Hang on then.

"We're heading down."

You did it, Dad.

My mom would've liked you.
I...
I am sure I would have liked her too.

Ouch.
How are you feeling, Victoria?
Oh, I'm fine. Just a scratch really.

All the responsibility here. In my hand.
I was thinking... maybe it's time I really used this brain of mine.
See if I can make something good out of all this.

I mean... I think I can do it.
I know you can.

I must go now. With my memory properly restored...
I have friends waiting for me. Responsibilities of my own.

Hey, stay in touch, okay?
I mean, in a strange kinda freaky way--
--we're family.
Family.

I have family.

Like *father*, like *son*.

—well into tomorrow.
PHINEAS T. HORTON
BRILLIANT SCIENTIST
BELOVED GRANDFATHER
END.

THE AVENGERS
APPROVED BY THE COMICS CODE AUTHORITY
MARVEL COMICS GROUP
12¢ IND.
57 OCT
BEHOLD... THE VISION!

THEN, SILENTLY, EFFORTLESSLY ...LIKE SOME GREAT, VENGEFUL BIRD OF PREY... HE SWOOPS INTO THE MOONLESS, CLOUD-DRAPED SKY...TOWARDS A TOWERING STRUCTURE NEARBY...

"BEHOLD...THE VISION!"

AN EERIE EXPEDITION INTO UNEXPLORED REALMS, CONDUCTED BY:
STAN LEE, EDITOR!
ROY THOMAS, WRITER!
JOHN BUSCEMA, ARTIST!
GEORGE KLEIN, INKER!
SAM ROSEN, LETTERER!

YES, MASTER! JUST THE SAME, I WISH YOU'D...
NO CAN DO, JAN... SORRY!
EVER TRY BREAKING A DATE WITH A WHOLE HERD OF BACTERIA? ---'NIGHT!
GOOD-NIGHT... HANK...

DARN IT!
OF ALL THE THINGS TO BE STOOD UP FOR---A BUNCH OF GERMS, NO LESS!
AND JUST WHEN I WAS SURE HANK WAS GOING TO PRO-POSE! I...

THAT SOUND---! SOMEONE JUST OPENED THE DOOR TO THE TERRACE!
CAN'T SEE YET, BUT I FEEL THE WIND... AND HIS PRESENCE!
WHO..?

2

YOUR TIME HAS COME, JANET VAN DYNE!
AND, THERE IS NOTHING YOU CAN DO... TO STAY YOUR FATE!
NO--NO! IT'S SOME SORT OF UNEARTHLY, INHUMAN VISION--!
AND THAT VOICE... LIKE SOMETHING FROM BEYOND THE GRAVE...!
KEEP YOUR HEAD, GIRL... YOU'VE BEEN THREATENED BEFORE!

DON'T KNOW WHO OR WHAT IS MENACING ME!
BUT MY WASP POWERS OFFER ME A SURE OUT!

MADE IT!
AND HOW MANY YOUNG LADIES CAN AVOID TROUBLE BY BEING SHRINKING VIOLETS?
OR BY TAKING A POWDER THRU A KEYHOLE?

SHOULD BE SAFE ENOUGH TO GROW AGAIN...THAT DOOR'S LOCKED, AND AN INCH THICK!
NOW TO CALL HANK, AND... WAIT!

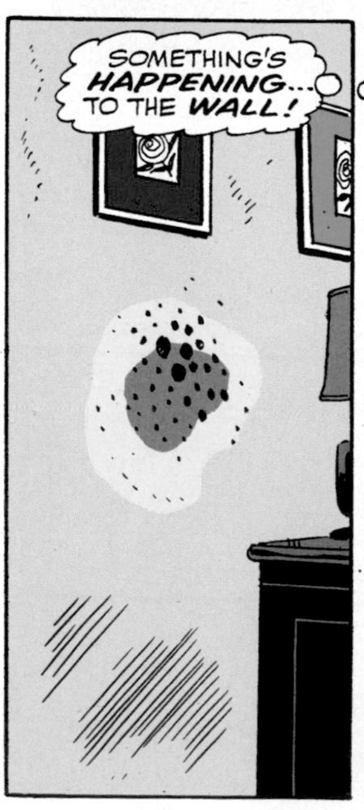
SOMETHING'S HAPPENING... TO THE WALL!

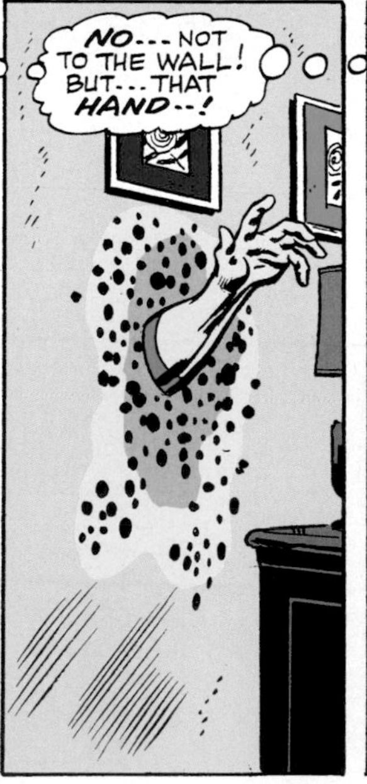
NO--- NOT TO THE WALL! BUT--- THAT HAND--!

THAT HORRIBLE THING...IS WALKING THRU THE WALL---AS IF IT WEREN'T THERE!

NO..NO! STAY BACK--!!
3.

NEXT, AS JAN INSTINCTIVELY TURNS TO FLEE...
DO WHAT YOU WILL, YOU WHO ARE CALLED THE WASP!
YOU CANNOT ESCAPE THE SEARING GAZE OF MY THERMO-SCOPIC EYES!
THAT HEAT... IT'S UN-BEARABLE..!
OR SOON SHALL BE... WHEN I INCREASE ITS UNIMAGINABLE POWER!
BUT THEN... WITHOUT WARN-ING...
AAARRHH!
THE PAIN-- INSIDE MY HEAD! CAN'T STAND IT--!
A MOMENT LATER, ON THE RAIN-DRENCHED STREETS BELOW...
THAT SIGNAL...
ACTIVATING THE TRANSCEIVER ON MY BELT...
IT'S JAN!
CAN'T WASTE TIME USING THE ELEVATOR!
GOT TO REACH HER FAST.. GOLIATH STYLE!
4

UH OH! FORGOT THAT NOT EVERYBODY'S USED TO SEEING GIANTS SCALING THEIR WALLS!
BUT, CAN'T WORRY ABOUT THAT NOW!
WAKE UP, MATILDA!
IT'S JUST A MIRAGE ...I THINK!
HERE'S JAN'S PENTHOUSE, ON THE TOP FLOOR! ONLY HOPE I'M IN TIME!
JAN! ARE YOU ALL RIGHT..?
I AM, LOVER MAN!
BUT I'VE GOT A WINDOW THAT'LL NEVER BE THE SAME AGAIN!
HUH? IS THAT ALL THE THANKS I GET FOR...
THANKS? FOR SMASHING THAT EXPENSIVE GLASS TO SMITHEREENS?
EVEN MY WOULD-BE ASSAILANT OPENED IT BY HAND!
OKAY, JAN BABY... SO YOU'RE ACTING LIKE A FIRST-RATE FINK!
STILL, YOU'VE GOTTA GET EVEN SOMEHOW FOR BEING WALKED OUT ON!
...EVEN IF YOU WERE SCARED STIFF JUST HALF A MINUTE AGO!
LOOK, LET'S GET DOWN TO CASES, HUH?
WHO--OR WHAT... IS THIS GUY?
AND, WHAT MADE HIM COLLAPSE IN A HEAP LIKE THAT?
FRANKLY, HE DOESN'T LOOK LIKE THE TYPE TO BE TAKEN OUT BY YOUR WASP'S STINGS!
I'M AS MUCH IN THE DARK AS YOU, HANK!
SO, WHY DON'T WE GIVE HIM THE ONCE-OVER AT AVENGERS HQ?
...AFTER YOU WRITE ME A CHECK FOR MY WINDOW, THAT IS!
5.

MEANWHILE, IN ANOTHER APARTMENT, SOMEWHERE ON NEW YORK'S UPPER EAST SIDE...
HI, 'TASH, HONEY! I GOT HERE AS FAST AS I---
WHAT IN BLAZES IS GOIN' ON HERE?

THERE'S NO NEED TO SHOUT, MY AMOROUS ARCHER!
YOU'VE SEEN THE BLACK WIDOW WALKING ON CEILINGS BEFORE!
MEBBE SO... BUT I DIDN'T THINK I WAS GONNA SEE IT AGAIN!
I THOUGHT YOU GAVE UP ALL THAT JAZZ--- FOR GOOD!

SO DID I...WHEN I COMPLETED MY LAST ASSIGNMENT FOR SHIELD!
BUT IT'S A LADY'S PREROGATIVE TO CHANGE HER MIND, IS IT NOT?
YA DON'T HAVETA TRY DAZZLIN OL' HAWKEYE WITH DOUBLE-TALK, LADY!
NICK FURY'S OFFERED YOU ANOTHER JOB...RIGHT?
THWOP!

AS A MATTER OF FACT...HE DID!
AND, SINCE YOU SEEM FOREVER TOO BUSY TO DO MORE THAN OCCASION-ALLY VISIT ME..!
YEAH, IF YOU CALL RISKIN' YOUR LIFE "BUSY"! I---
YOU SEE? I MIGHT AS WELL BE BACK IN SIBERIA..!
YEESH! THERE GOES MY BELT SIGNAL!
NOW WADDA THEY WANT?
BZZZZ

NOT NOW, NATASHA, HUH?
HAWKEYE HERE! WHAT'S UP, MAN-MOUNTAIN..?
I KIND'A THOUGHT YOU WERE GONNA SAY THAT!
NO, DON'T SWEAT IT! I'M ON MY WAY!
BUT, YOU SURE KNOW HOW TO THROW A DAMPER ON A GUY'S LOVE LIFE!
WHAT LOVE LIFE? IT'S BEEN WEEKS SINCE WE EVEN HAD DINNER TOGETHER!
I'M SURE THAT MY NEW ASSIGN-MENT FOR SHIELD WILL BE AT LEAST THAT ROMANTIC!
6

LOOK, I DON'T HAVE TIME TO MINCE WORDS WITH YA RIGHT NOW, DOLL!
WE'LL TALK ABOUT IT AFTER I ANSWER THAT EMERGENCY CALL, OKAY?
WHAT IS THERE TO DISCUSS?
WHEN YOU RETURN... I'LL NO LONGER BE HERE!

MEANWHILE, ON ANOTHER RAIN-SWEPT STREET SOME BLOCKS NORTH---
HAD TO GET OUT OF THE AVENGERS' MANSION!
ONLY HERE, IN THE OPEN AIR, CAN THE BLACK PANTHER BE FREE TO THINK---
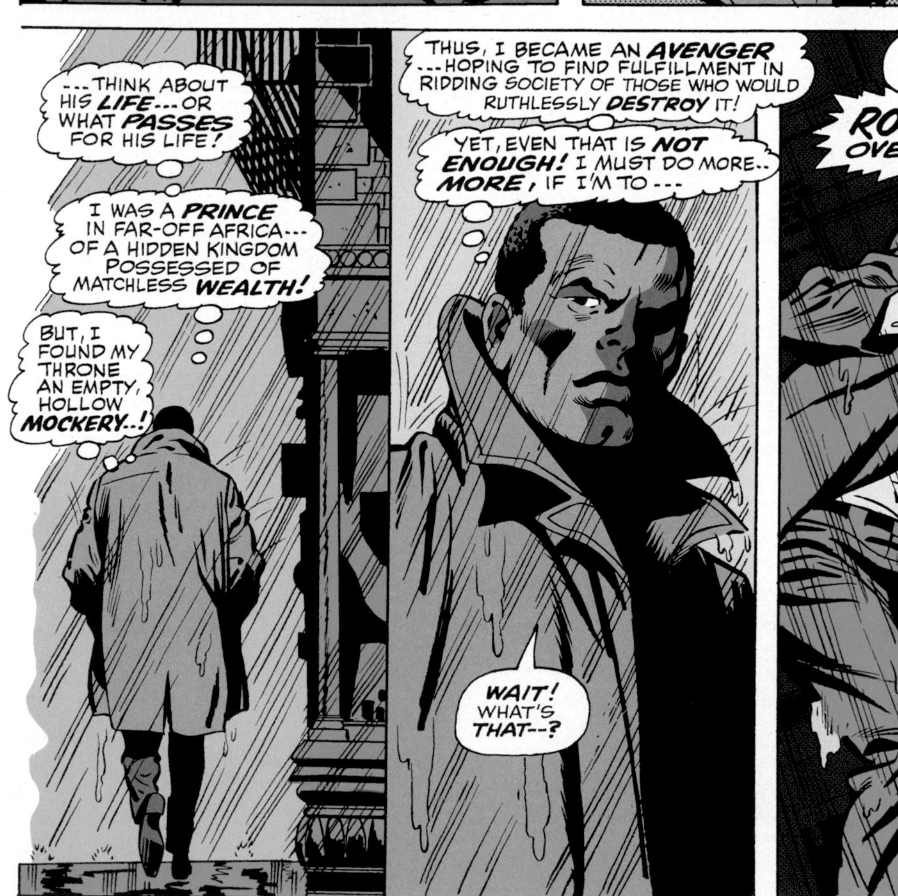
---THINK ABOUT HIS LIFE---OR WHAT PASSES FOR HIS LIFE!
I WAS A PRINCE IN FAR-OFF AFRICA--- OF A HIDDEN KINGDOM POSSESSED OF MATCHLESS WEALTH!
BUT, I FOUND MY THRONE AN EMPTY, HOLLOW MOCKERY..!
THUS, I BECAME AN AVENGER ---HOPING TO FIND FULFILLMENT IN RIDDING SOCIETY OF THOSE WHO WOULD RUTHLESSLY DESTROY IT!
YET, EVEN THAT IS NOT ENOUGH! I MUST DO MORE.. MORE, IF I'M TO---
WAIT! WHAT'S THAT--?

HELP... POLICE!
ROBBERY... OVER THERE!
7.

THAT'S ONE CREEP WON'T BE DOIN' ANY MORE SQUEALIN' FOR A WHILE!
I WINGED 'IM IN THE LEG!
YEAH...AFTER HE BLEW THE WHISTLE ON US!
WHAT'S THE DIFF?
IN THIS DOWN-POUR, WHO'S GONNA STOP US?

MEBBE SO...BUT I AIN'T GONNA HANG AROUND TO TAKE A SURVEY!
GET IN, TRIGGER-HAPPY...OR I'M CUTTIN' OUT BY MYSELF!
DON'T GET YER JAWS IN AN UPROAR, TURK!
NOBODY SAW US BUT ONE GUY IN A RAINCOAT...AND WHAT'S HE GONNA DO?

SOMETIMES, MY FRIEND, ONE MAN CAN DO QUITE A BIT...
IF HE MERELY SETS HIS MIND TO IT!
AARRRHH!
IT'S..THAT PANTHER GUY!

AND NOW, BECAUSE YOU GENTS SEEM RATHER THE IMPATIENT TYPE...
I'LL LET MY FISTS DO THE REST OF MY PHILO-SOPHIZING FOR ME!
MMMFF!
8

...AND YOU SET THE WOUNDED GUY'S LEG IN A SPLINT, TOO...EH, PANTHER?
SO AM I, OFFICER!
GLAD TO SEE YOU AVENGERS HAVE TIME TO DO SOMETHING BESIDES SAVE THE EARTH FROM SUPER-VILLAINS ONCE IN A WHILE!
NOW, IF YOU'LL EXCUSE ME, THERE'S SOME-THING I MUST DO..!
MAN, THAT BLACK PANTHER IS SOME-THIN' ELSE!
WE COULD SURE USE 'IM ON MY BLOCK!
SOMETHING IN THAT YOUNGSTER'S VOICE MAY JUST HAVE GIVEN ME THE ANSWER I'VE BEEN SEEKING!*
BUT FIRST, IT'S TIME THAT I CHECKED IN, TO SEE IF...
SORRY, HANK... DIDN'T HEAR YOUR SIGNAL... TOO PRE-OCCUPIED, I GUESS!
I'LL BE THERE IN TEN MINUTES!
*AN ANSWER, HOWEVER, WHICH WILL HAVE TO WAIT FOR AN ISH OR TWO! --SNEAKY STAN.
...I STILL DON'T SEE WHY YOU CAN'T TELL ME IF MY VISITOR WAS HUMAN OR NOT, HIGH-POCKETS!
PERHAPS IT'S BECAUSE ...HE WAS BOTH, JAN!
EXACTLY, T'CHALLA!
ACCORDING TO MY EXAMINATION, HE'S EVERY INCH A HUMAN BEING...
...EXCEPT THAT ALL HIS BODILY ORGANS ARE CONSTRUCTED OF SYNTHETIC MATERIALS!
HOLY CATS, MAN-MOUNTAIN... LIKE YOUR SYNTHOZOID!
THE WHAT, HAWKEYE? I DON'T...
A SYNTHOZOID, PANTHER... A NAME I ONCE COINED FOR AN ARTIFICIAL HUMAN!
HAWKEYE REMEMBERS THAT I USED TO BE TRYING TO DEVELOP SUCH A THING, BUT I NEVER...
WAIT! HE'S STARTING TO MOVE... TO BREATHE AGAIN!
--THOUGH I STILL CAN'T GUESS WHAT MADE HIM STOP!
9

WHERE AM I? WHAT HAPPENED TO..?
WAIT...NOW I REMEMBER MY MISSION...
A MISSION TO KILL!
WHO ARE YOU, AND WHY..?

I? PERHAPS I AM WHAT THE WASP CALLED ME... A VISION!
A VISION OF DEATH... FOR THE AVENGERS!
HUH? WHAT KIND'A NUT ARE YOU, ANYWAY?
TO COIN A CLICHÉ... WE GOT YOU SURROUNDED, PAL!

TO SURROUND ONE SUCH AS I MAY BE A SIMPLE MATTER, AVENGERS!
BUT IT IS QUITE ANOTHER THING...
RRIPP

...TO SURVIVE SUCH SEEMING SUCCESS!
HE'S GOT THE STRENGTH OF AN ARMY!
HAD TO DO SOME PLAIN AND FANCY GROWING...
...OR HE'D HAVE MADE HIS THREAT COME TRUE!

GOOD STOP, TALL SOCKS! NOW IT'S OUR T...
HEY! WHAT IN...?
UNNHH!
HE SEEMS SO MASSIVE... SOLID ENOUGH FOR TWO MEN..!
10

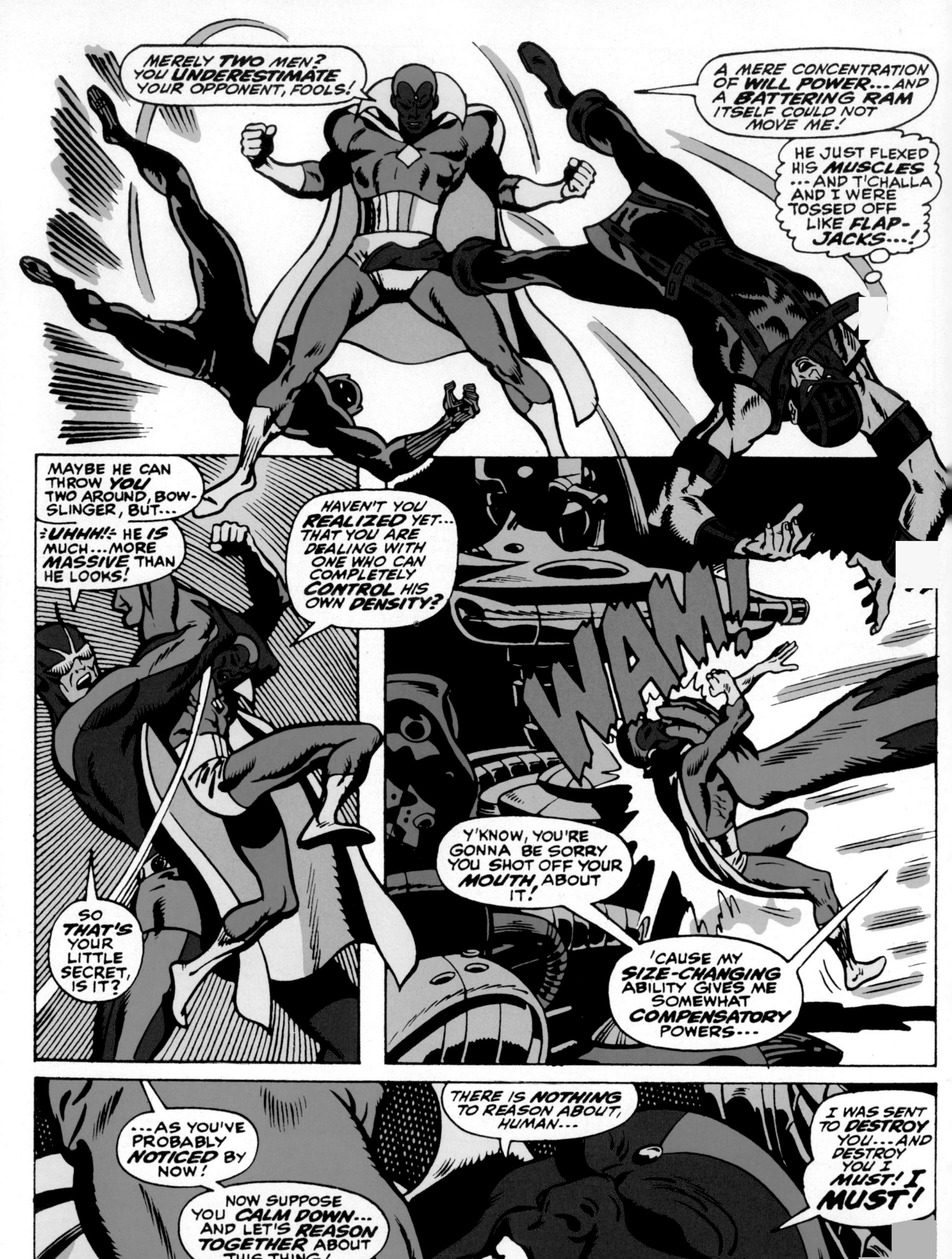
MERELY TWO MEN? YOU UNDERESTIMATE YOUR OPPONENT, FOOLS!
A MERE CONCENTRATION OF WILL POWER... AND A BATTERING RAM ITSELF COULD NOT MOVE ME!
HE JUST FLEXED HIS MUSCLES ... AND T'CHALLA AND I WERE TOSSED OFF LIKE FLAP-JACKS...!
MAYBE HE CAN THROW YOU TWO AROUND, BOW-SLINGER, BUT...
UHHH! HE IS MUCH... MORE MASSIVE THAN HE LOOKS!
HAVEN'T YOU REALIZED YET... THAT YOU ARE DEALING WITH ONE WHO CAN COMPLETELY CONTROL HIS OWN DENSITY?
SO THAT'S YOUR LITTLE SECRET, IS IT?
WAM!
Y'KNOW, YOU'RE GONNA BE SORRY YOU SHOT OFF YOUR MOUTH ABOUT IT!
'CAUSE MY SIZE-CHANGING ABILITY GIVES ME SOMEWHAT COMPENSATORY POWERS...
...AS YOU'VE PROBABLY NOTICED BY NOW!
NOW SUPPOSE YOU CALM DOWN... AND LET'S REASON TOGETHER ABOUT THIS THING!
THERE IS NOTHING TO REASON ABOUT, HUMAN...
I WAS SENT TO DESTROY YOU... AND DESTROY YOU I MUST! I MUST!
11.

STRANGE... HE SPEAKS LIKE A MAN... OR AN ANDROID... IN A TRANCE!
HE TALKS ABOUT HAVING TO TRY TO KILL US... YET MAKES NO MOVE!
MAYBE THAT PUTS YOUR MIND AT EASE, JUNGLE MAN...
BROTHER HAWKEYE'S STILL GONNA SCOOP UP HIS ARROWS!
I DON'T GET IT! FROM WHAT YOU TOLD ME, JAN...
...HE COULD WALK OUT OF THIS ROOM... AT WILL!
WHO ARE YOU, FELLA?
HOW'D YOU GET SUCH POWERS?
YOU NEED NOT BELIEVE ME, ARCHER...
BUT, IN TRUTH... I DO NOT KNOW!
IF ONLY... I COULD REMEMBER--!
YOU'VE GOT TO REMEMBER, VISION... SO WE CAN BE FRIENDS, NOT DEADLY ENEMIES!
I, TOO, FEEL WE SHOULD BE... ALLIES!
AND YET, A DARK MIST CLOUDS MY MIND, SO THAT...
WAIT! SUDDENLY, I RECALL ---
...RECALL THE ONE WHO CREATED ME... ORDERED ME TO DESTROY YOU!
IT WAS A METAL BEING... WHO CALLED HIMSELF ULTRON-5!
I SEE FROM YOUR FACES THAT YOU, ALSO, HAVE HEARD THAT NAME BEFORE!
I DON'T KNOW WHY... BUT THE MERE REMEMBRANCE OF IT FILLS ME WITH A FEELING OF... HATRED!
...IF A CREATURE SUCH AS I BE ALLOWED TO HAVE EMOTIONS!
12.

IT IS UNCANNY... BUT, NOW THAT I HAVE PLUMBED MY DIM MEMORIES BACK AS FAR AS THEY WILL GO...
I NO LONGER FEEL ANY DESIRE TO ATTACK YOU!
IN FACT, IF YOU WISH.. I'LL LEAD YOU TO HIM WHO... CREATED ME!
WE'VE BEEN HUNTING THAT METAL MANIAC FOR WEEKS!
SO, WE'VE GOT TO TAKE A CHANCE ON YOU!
STILL, JUST IN CASE THERE'S SOME TRICK UP YOUR SLEEVE...
I'M KEEPIN' A SHOCK ARROW TRAINED RIGHT ON YOUR SYNTHETIC KISSER!

MOMENTS LATER, A SLEEK AIR-CRUISER SOARS INTO THE SKY... ITS OCCUPANTS CLOAKED IN SOMBRE SILENCE...

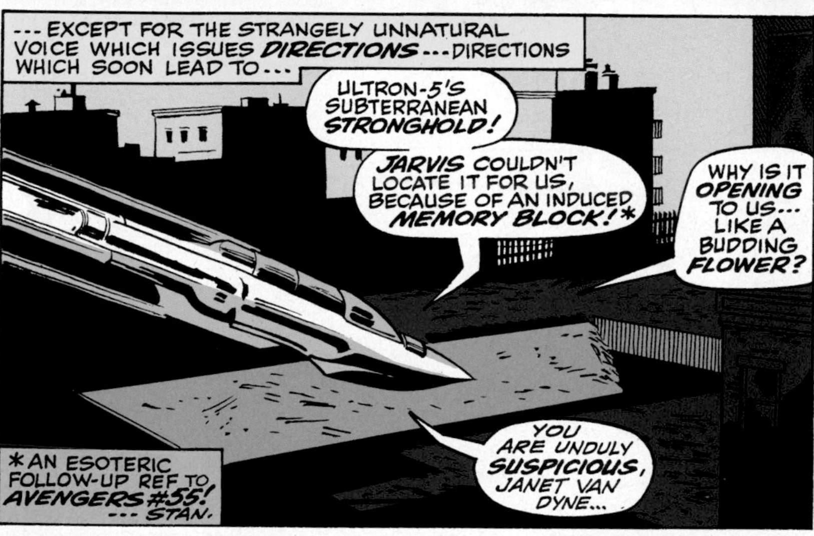
--- EXCEPT FOR THE STRANGELY UNNATURAL VOICE WHICH ISSUES DIRECTIONS --- DIRECTIONS WHICH SOON LEAD TO ...
ULTRON-5'S SUBTERRANEAN STRONGHOLD!
JARVIS COULDN'T LOCATE IT FOR US, BECAUSE OF AN INDUCED MEMORY BLOCK!*
WHY IS IT OPENING TO US... LIKE A BUDDING FLOWER?
YOU ARE UNDULY SUSPICIOUS, JANET VAN DYNE...
*AN ESOTERIC FOLLOW-UP REF TO AVENGERS #55! --- STAN.

---REMEMBER, MY CREATOR'S PROTECTIVE DEVICES WERE SET TO RE-ADMIT ME!
SPEAKING OF YOUR SUPPOSED CREATOR---
JUST WHO IS HE... AND WHY IS HE SO FANATICAL ABOUT DESTROYING THE AVENGERS?
THAT, GOLIATH, EVEN I DO NOT KNOW...
13

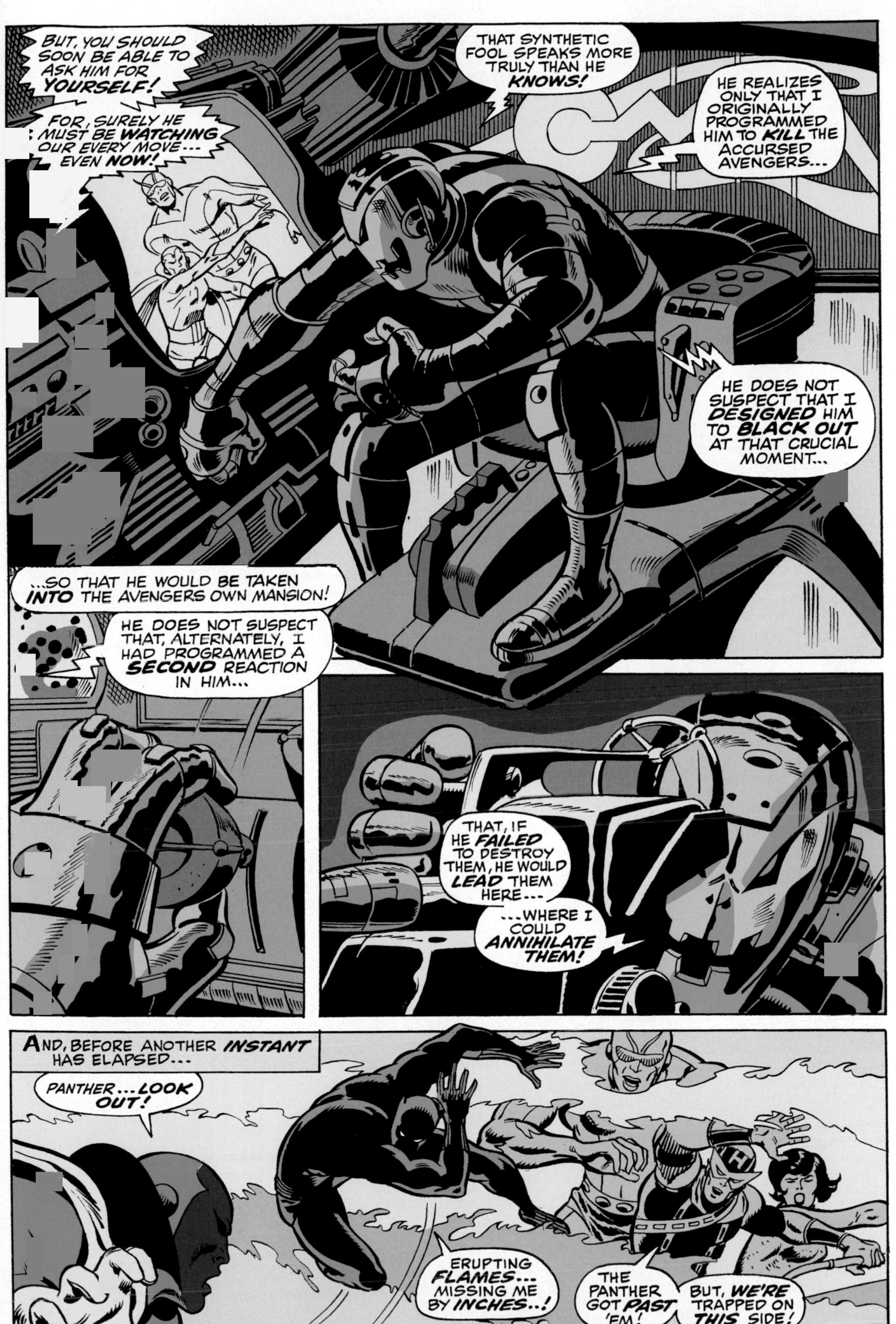
BUT, YOU SHOULD SOON BE ABLE TO ASK HIM FOR YOURSELF!
FOR, SURELY HE MUST BE WATCHING OUR EVERY MOVE--- EVEN NOW!
THAT SYNTHETIC FOOL SPEAKS MORE TRULY THAN HE KNOWS!
HE REALIZES ONLY THAT I ORIGINALLY PROGRAMMED HIM TO KILL THE ACCURSED AVENGERS...
HE DOES NOT SUSPECT THAT I DESIGNED HIM TO BLACK OUT AT THAT CRUCIAL MOMENT...
...SO THAT HE WOULD BE TAKEN INTO THE AVENGERS OWN MANSION!
HE DOES NOT SUSPECT THAT, ALTERNATELY, I HAD PROGRAMMED A SECOND REACTION IN HIM...
THAT, IF HE FAILED TO DESTROY THEM, HE WOULD LEAD THEM HERE---
---WHERE I COULD ANNIHILATE THEM!
AND, BEFORE ANOTHER INSTANT HAS ELAPSED...
PANTHER...LOOK OUT!
ERUPTING FLAMES... MISSING ME BY INCHES..!
THE PANTHER GOT PAST 'EM!
BUT, WE'RE TRAPPED ON THIS SIDE!
14

UH OH! LOOKS LIKE I TALKED OUTTA TURN!
WHAT ELSE IS NEW, BOW-SLINGER?
SOON AS YOU TWO ARE OVER, I'LL SHOOT UP TO 25 FEET, AND...
AAARRHH!
ONE SUDDEN, SINKING MOMENT LATER... EVEN AS HANK PYM'S MIGHTY FRAME LANDS DOZENS OF FEET BELOW... A HULKING FORM LOOMS OVER HIM, ITS IN-HUMAN FACE A MASK OF LETHAL MENACE..!
I DON'T KNOW IF THAT'S A ROBOT... A SYNTHO-ZOID... OR WHAT... BUT IT SURE ISN'T HEADING MY WAY TO SHAKE MY HAND!
ULTRON-5 HAS MORE KINDS OF ANDROIDS THAN ANDY WARHOL HAS SOUP CANS!
WORSE... THAT FALL SHOOK ME UP SO BAD... CAN'T CONCENTRATE ON CHANGING SIZE!
MAYBE... I CAN FAKE HIM OUT... GET PAST HIM...!
BUT, FAR MORE SWIFTLY THAN GOLIATH COULD HAVE GUESSED...
THOK!
WITH ONE BLOW ..HE KNOCKED EVERY BIT OF WIND OUT OF ME...!
15

LOOKS LIKE...I'VE HAD IT...
WHAM!
WELL DONE, LACKEY! NOW, BRING THE GIANT ONE TO ME...AT CONTROL CENTER!
ONE AVENGER HAS FALLEN---BUT THREE YET REMAIN--!
...I DON'T LIKE IT, HAWKEYE!
THE WAY HANK VANISHED--- IT HAD ALL THE MARKINGS OF A WELL-LAID TRAP!
WADDA YOU SAY ABOUT IT, VISION?
THAT IS ALL THE MORE REASON FOR YOU TO FOLLOW ME---TO BEARD ULTRON-5 IN HIS LAIR, BEFORE...
BUT HANK--- WHAT ABOUT HANK?
HE MAY NEED OUR HELP--!
THWIK!
THAT'S RIGHT, CLOWNS!
STAND THERE, THE VICTIM OF YOUR OWN INANE EMOTIONS!
THE BETTER FOR ME TO KILL YOU WITH!
I KNOW HOW YA FEEL, JAN---
BUT, YOU GOTTA SEE THIS WAY IS BEST! YOU GOTTA...
IT'S NOT LIKE THAT, KID---I SWEAR IT'S NOT!
I ONLY SEE...THAT YOU MAY BE LEAVING HANK---TO DIE!
OHHH... LOOK! THE WALLS--!
THEY'RE CLOSING IN ON US!
IT WAS A TRAP... THE WHOLE BIT!
I DID NOT KNOW... I DIDN'T!
THEN HELP US SMASH THESE WALLS... BEFORE IT'S TOO LATE!
16

I...CAN'T..!
THEY'RE CONSTRUCTED OF AN ALLOY SO STRONG... SO IRRESISTIBLE... THAT, EVEN AT MY GREATEST DENSITY...
IT WOULD ONLY BE A MATTER OF TIME BEFORE I, TOO, WOULD BE CRUSHED... ALONG WITH YOU!

AND, IT WOULDN'T BE NICE TO GET YOUR OWN SYNTHETIC SELF SQUASHED LIKE A BUG, WOULD IT?
SO NATURALLY, YOU'VE GOTTA CUT OUT ON US... GO LOOKIN' FOR ULTRON-5 BY YOUR LONESOME!
EASY, HAWKEYE! THAT MAY WELL BE THE BEST COURSE... IF HE TELLS THE TRUTH!
THEN NONE OF YOU REALLY TRUSTS ME!
BUT, I SHALL PROVE MY WORTH... BY DEFEATING HIM WHO MADE ME!
IF YOU DON'T DO IT FAST, COME BACK LATER AN' SCRAPE US OFF THE WALLS, HUH?

THE EMBITTERED BOWMAN WAS CORRECT!
THOUGH THE WALLS MOVE SLOWLY... THEY MOVE REMORSELESSLY!
THEY MUST BE RESCUED SWIFTLY... OR NOT AT ALL!
YET, THEY WERE MUCH NEARER THAN THEY KNEW...
...TO THE NERVE CENTER OF THIS SINISTER BEEHIVE!
SO... YOU'VE RETURNED TO YOUR SENSES, AT LAST!
YOU WERE WISE, ANDROID... WISE TO THUS DESERT THE DOOMED MORTALS!

WELL, DO NOT SIMPLY STAND THERE... LIKE SOME LIFELESS MANNEQUIN!
I GAVE YOU A TONGUE TO SPEAK... LET ME HEAR YOUR REPORT!
YES... YOU CREATED ME... GAVE ME LIFE!
BUT, YOU MEANT ME TO BE NOTHING BUT A NAMELESS, SOULLESS IMITATION OF A HUMAN BEING!
RELEASE THE AVENGERS ...OR FACE HIM WHOM THEY HAVE NAMED ...THE VISION!
WHAT? YOU DARE TO CHALLENGE ME...??
17.

FOR THAT, I SHOULD DESTROY YOU... REND YOU LIMB FROM L---
YET, WHY SHOULD WE QUARREL...
...WE, WHO ARE BOTH SO FAR ABOVE THE GROVELING HUMAN RACE?
IF YOU WISH THE AVENGERS TO BE SPARED---SO SHALL IT BE!
WHAT MEAN A FEW HUMAN LIVES TO ULTRON-5?
WHY THIS SUDDEN CHANGE OF HEART, EVIL ONE?
THEN, THE VISION HAS HIS SURPRISING ANSWER...
AARRHH!
ULTRON-5 DOES NOT CHANGE HIS MIND---
...AND HAS NOT EVEN AN ARTIFICIAL HEART, AS YOU DO---!
BUT, REALIZING THAT I HAD CREATED YOU WITH SUCH GREAT POWERS...
I KNEW I COULD ONLY DEFEAT YOU--- BY LOWERING YOUR GUARD!
MY SOLE WEAKNESS IS THE TWIN ELECTRODES WHICH STUD THE SIDE OF MY METALLIC SKULL---
...WHILE YOU RUN THE PITIFUL GAMUT OF EMOTIONS--- INCLUDING THAT OF TRUST!
AND NOW, DIE, FOOL---DIE AS YOU SHOULD HAVE DIED BEFORE!!
YET, INCREDIBLY...
YOU LIVE! BUT HOW...
WHEN I HURLED YOU STUNNED--BODILY-- INTO THAT SEETH-ING ENERGY VAT!?
WHAT CANNOT BE TOUCHED ---CANNOT BE HARMED!
I REDUCED MY DENSITY TO NEARLY ZERO AT THE LAST POSSIBLE INSTANT!
18

BUT NOW, BEFORE YOU RELEASE THE AVENGERS, YOU MUST ANSWER THE QUESTION WHICH BURNS IN MY MIND!
I HAVE HUMAN THOUGHTS... HUMAN MEMORIES!
WHY, ULTRON-5? WHO... OR WHAT... AM I??
THAT YOU SHALL NEVER KNOW, WRETCHED ONE... BECAUSE I DO NOT CHOOSE TO TELL YOU!
RATHER, I CHOOSE NOW---

...TO DESTROY Y... WHA..?
YOU RIDICULED ME FOR HAVING EMOTIONS---YET YOU POSSESS THEM NO LESS THAN I!
OR ELSE YOU WOULD NOT HAVE LEAPED AT ME IN YOUR RAGE..

---TO YOUR OWN UTTER ANNIHILATION!
FWOOOM!
NO... NO! AAARRH!

GONE IN ONE SHATTERING INSTANT IS THE MYSTERIOUS, SINISTER THREAT OF ULTRON-5... AND, IN THAT SELFSAME MOMENT---
THE WALLS HAVE STOPPED---IN THE PROVERBIAL NICK!
THEN, THE VISION WAS ON OUR SIDE---AND HE SUCCEEDED!
IT HAS TO BE!
MY ROBOT CAPTOR COLLAPSED... LIKE A PUPPET WITH CLIPPED STRINGS!
SOMETHING HAPPENED... BUT WHAT?

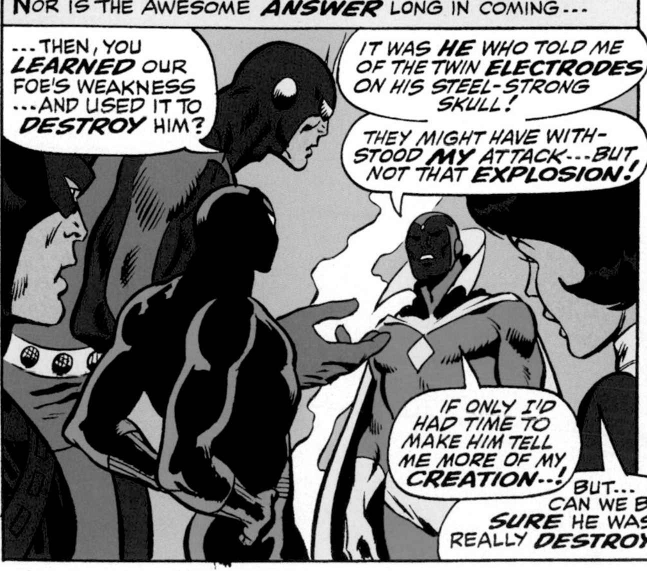
NOR IS THE AWESOME ANSWER LONG IN COMING...
...THEN, YOU LEARNED OUR FOE'S WEAKNESS ...AND USED IT TO DESTROY HIM?
IT WAS HE WHO TOLD ME OF THE TWIN ELECTRODES ON HIS STEEL-STRONG SKULL!
THEY MIGHT HAVE WITHSTOOD MY ATTACK---BUT NOT THAT EXPLOSION!
IF ONLY I'D HAD TIME TO MAKE HIM TELL ME MORE OF MY CREATION--!
BUT... CAN WE BE SURE HE WAS REALLY DESTROYED?

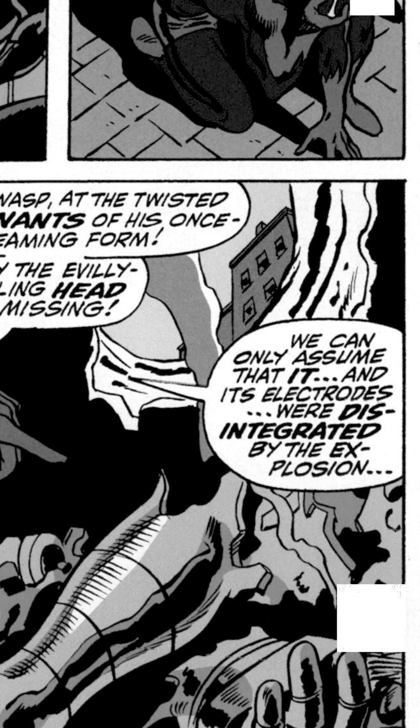
LOOK, WASP, AT THE TWISTED REMNANTS OF HIS ONCE-GLEAMING FORM!
ONLY THE EVILLY-SMILING HEAD IS MISSING!
WE CAN ONLY ASSUME THAT IT... AND ITS ELECTRODES ...WERE DISINTEGRATED BY THE EXPLOSION...
19

EPILOGUE:

I met a traveler from
an antique land,
Who said:

Two vast and trunkless
legs of stone
Stand in the desert.

Near them, on the sand,
Half sunk, a shattered
visage lies,

Whose frown,
And wrinkled lip, and sneer
of cold command,

Tell that its sculptor well
those passions read
Which yet survive, stamped
on these lifeless things...

The hand that mocked them,
and the heart that fed;
And on the pedestal these
words appear:

"My name is Ozymandias,
King of Kings:
Look on my works, ye
Mighty, and despair!"

Nothing beside remains.
Round the decay
Of that colossal wreck,
Boundless and bare

The lone and level sands
stretch far away.

AVENGERS
MARVEL COMICS GROUP
APPROVED BY THE COMICS CODE AUTHORITY
25¢
135
MAY
02458
EARTH'S MIGHTIEST HEROES!
the AVENGERS
--AND NOW ULTRON-5 WILL DESTROY YOU!
IT WAS ULTRON-5 WHO CREATED YOU, ANDROID--
JOURNEY THRU TIME WITH EARTH'S MIGHTIEST HEROES TO LEARN THE SHATTERING SECRET OF MANTIS...PLUS--
How the HUMAN TORCH became... THE VISION!

GIANT-SIZE AVENGERS

4 JUNE 02922

50¢

CC

68 BIG PAGES

MARVEL COMICS GROUP™

APPROVED BY THE COMICS CODE AUTHORITY

GIANT-SIZE AVENGERS™

NEW!

AVENGERS ASSEMBLE-- FOR THE MOST LONG-AWAITED **WEDDING** OF THE DECADE!

BUT WHAT GOD HAS JOINED TOGETHER-- *THE DREAD DORMAMMU* MAY PUT ASUNDER!

MARVEL®

The West Coas
Avengers™

VisionQuest™ CONTINUES

75¢ US
95¢ CAN
45
JUN
02100

BEHOLD THE VISION!™

BYRNE after BUSCEMA & KLEIN